D1586489

# EATING OUT
## ...at home

**over 60 low Point recipes for your restaurant and take away favourites**

SIMON & SCHUSTER
A VIACOM COMPANY

**Tamsin Burnett-Hall**

First published in Great Britain by Simon & Schuster UK Ltd, 2004
A Viacom Company

Simon & Schuster UK Ltd
Africa House
64–78 Kingsway
London
WC2B 6AH

Photography by Iain Bagwell
Styling by Rachel Jukes
Food preparation by Penny Stephens

Design by Jane Humphrey
Typesetting by Stylize Digital Artwork
Printed and bound in China

Weight Watchers Publications Manager: Corrina Griffin
Weight Watchers Publications Executives: Lucy Davidson,
Mandy Spittle
Weight Watchers Publications Assistant: Nina Bhogal

A CIP catalogue for this book is available from the British Library

ISBN  07432 484 65

Pictured on the front cover: Pad Thai Noodles, page 51

Pictured on the back cover: Frutti di Bosco Cheesecake, page 32

Raw Eggs: Only the freshest eggs should be used. Pregnant
women, the elderly and children should avoid recipes with
eggs which are not fully cooked or raw.

All fruits, vegetables and eggs are medium size unless otherwise
stated.

Recipe timings are approximate and meant to be guidelines.
Please note that the preparation time includes all the steps
up to and following the main cooking time(s).

 You'll find this easy to read logo on every recipe
throughout the book. The logo represents the
number of Points per serving each recipe contains.
The easy to use Points system is designed to help
you eat what you want, when you want – as long
as you stay within your Points allowance – giving
you the freedom to enjoy the food you love.

**V** This symbol denotes a vegetarian recipe and
assumes vegetarian cheese and free range eggs
are used. Virtually fat free fromage frais and low
fat crème fraîche may contain traces of gelatine
so they are not always vegetarian: please check
the labels.

**Vg** This symbol denotes a vegan dish.

# contents

# restaurant style food
## ...for far

So, it's Friday night and you can't bear the thought of missing out on your favourite take away or evening out, but you're trying to lose weight and haven't saved up enough Points... well, there is another solution – you can still eat the foods you love, safe in the knowledge that you are sticking to your Points, by cooking one of the delicious recipes in *Eating Out At Home*.

It's usually very hard to make sensible low Point choices when picking up a take away or nipping out for a quick meal at a local pub or restaurant as most menus are not designed with a Points conscious Weight Watcher in mind. Often, even if we try to choose a sensible option, such as a chicken salad, it's only to find that it comes smothered in a creamy dressing that wasn't even mentioned on the menu.

Cooking at home puts you back in control of what you are eating. The recipes in this book recreate your favourite restaurant and take away dishes with a few clever tricks to dramatically lower the Points. This also means that you'll get a more generously sized portion than you would with a take away or a ready meal version. Cutting out the fat doesn't mean cutting out the flavour – far from it. You can safely serve up these recipes to friends and family without them even realising that they are eating so-called "diet" food – in fact they'll love you for it!

# fewer Points

People lead very busy lives, either working or running a family (or often both!), so they may not have a great deal of time to prepare meals. That's why over half of the recipes in this book can be on the table in 30 minutes or less, and some are ready in just 15 minutes – definitely less time than it takes to order and collect a take away. And then there's the added benefit of knowing that it will be much healthier for you, as well as a good deal cheaper.

You'll find plenty of recipes here for one or two people, while vegetarians are also well catered for, as two thirds of the recipes are either designed with vegetarians in mind or have vegetarian alternatives. The recipes are all easy to follow, using simple cooking techniques and readily available ingredients – even the exotic ones. If there is an ingredient which you haven't come across before, just ask an assistant at the supermarket to point you in the right direction and have fun experimenting! Trying out new recipes and flavour combinations provides variation in eating patterns and can help to keep you on track with your weight loss because you won't get bored eating the same few dishes all the time.

The Weight Watchers *Time To Eat* Programme is designed to fit around your life, and not the other way round, and this book is here to help you cook and eat the foods you love. So don't miss out on your favourite recipes – enjoy food and enjoy life!

# bistro

Bistro style food is traditionally found in little restaurants and cafés all over France and is now popular in bars and pubs here and across the Channel. Rather than being complicated, fancy restaurant-style dishes, these recipes are informal, and made from a few simple ingredients that are full of flavour and quick to prepare.

## MOULES PROVENÇALES

**3 Points per recipe**

*Serves 1*
*Preparation time and cooking time: 10 minutes*
*Calories per serving: 294*
*Freezing: not recommended*

Mussels in their shells are very easy and quick to cook, and because they take longer to eat they seem very filling! This tomato based sauce is full of the flavours of the Mediterranean, so make sure you've got a spoon ready to scoop up all the goodness! Serve with a medium crusty bread roll for an extra 2 Points.

1 teaspoon of olive oil

1 small onion, chopped finely

1 stick celery, sliced

1 small courgette, diced

1 garlic clove, sliced

230 g can chopped tomatoes with herbs

500 g (1 lb 2 oz) cleaned mussels (see tip)

salt and freshly ground black pepper

**1** Heat the olive oil in a large saucepan, add the onion and cook for 2 minutes, then add the celery, courgette and garlic and cook for a further 2 minutes.

**2** Add the tinned tomatoes, 3 tablespoons of water, the mussels and some seasoning. Toss the mussels around in the sauce then cover the pan and cook for 5 minutes over a moderate heat, shaking the pan a couple of times until the mussels have opened. Discard any mussels that stay closed after cooking.

**3** Tip into a deep warmed bowl to serve and have another bowl ready to put the empty shells in as you eat.

**Top tip** To clean mussels, scrub them in a sinkful of cold water and pull away the thread-like 'beard'. Discard any mussels that don't close when given a sharp tap or that don't open during cooking.

**Moules Provençales: Succulent mussels in a Mediterranean tomato sauce for just 3 Points per serving.**

Smoked Haddock
and Prawn
Fishcakes: Crisp-
coated fishcakes
served with a
delicious tartare
sauce, all for just 4
Points per serving.

## SMOKED HADDOCK AND PRAWN FISHCAKES

**16 Points per recipe**

Serves 4

Preparation time: 25 minutes + 1 hour chilling

Cooking time: 20 minutes

Calories per serving: 312

Freezing: not recommended

Smoked haddock gives these chunky textured fishcakes a fantastic flavour. Serve with a crisp, mixed No Point salad and a wedge of lemon.

450 g (1 lb) potatoes, peeled and diced

350 g (12 oz) smoked haddock

125 g (4½ oz) small prawns, defrosted

2 tablespoons chopped fresh parsley

1 tablespoon lemon juice

4 tablespoons skimmed milk

pinch cayenne pepper

1 egg, beaten

60 g (2 oz) natural dried breadcrumbs

low fat cooking spray

salt and freshly ground black pepper

**For the tartare sauce**

150 g tub 0% fat Greek yogurt

1 tablespoon low fat mayonnaise

4 cornichons (baby gherkins), diced

1 tablespoon capers, rinsed and chopped

½ tablespoon lemon juice

1 Boil the potatoes in salted water for 15 minutes or until tender, then drain and mash.

2 Place the smoked haddock in a pan of water and bring to the boil, then cover and poach for 5 minutes. Remove from the water and leave to cool, then flake the flesh.

3 Mix the mashed potatoes and flaked fish with the prawns, parsley, lemon juice, 2 tablespoons of the milk, cayenne pepper and seasoning. Chill the mixture in the fridge for 1 hour.

4 Preheat the oven to Gas Mark 4/ 180°C/fan oven 160°C. Beat the egg with the remaining milk and pour into a shallow dish. Tip the breadcrumbs onto a plate. Shape the fish and potato mixture into eight fishcakes and dip each one first in the egg mixture and then in the breadcrumbs to coat.

5 Heat a non-stick frying pan on the hob and spray with low fat cooking spray. Cook the fishcakes for 2 minutes on each side until lightly browned then transfer to a baking sheet and cook in the oven for 15 minutes.

6 Mix together the ingredients for the tartare sauce and serve with the hot fishcakes.

**Variation** You can use 60 g (2 oz) polenta or cornmeal to coat the fishcakes instead of the breadcrumbs if you like a crunchy coating. The Points per serving will then be 4½.

## CHICKEN LIVER PÂTÉ

**10½ Points per recipe**

Serves 4

Preparation and cooking time: 30 minutes soaking + 10 minutes + 2 hours chilling

Calories per serving: 139

Freezing: recommended

Try this deliciously smooth pâté spread on crisp Melba toast (1 Point for 6) as a starter. Alternatively, serve with No Point pickled cornichons (little gherkins) or silverskin onions as a light lunch.

250 g (9 oz) chicken livers, defrosted if frozen, rinsed

100 ml (3½ fl oz) skimmed milk, to cover

2 teaspoons half fat butter

1 small garlic clove, crushed

1 tablespoon chopped fresh thyme plus a few sprigs to garnish

2 tablespoons brandy

200 g tub extra light cream cheese

salt and freshly ground black pepper

1 Soak the chicken livers in milk for 30 minutes to remove any bitterness, then discard the milk and pat the livers dry on kitchen paper.

2 Heat a non-stick frying pan over a moderate heat. Melt the half fat butter in the pan, then add the chicken livers and stir-fry for 3 minutes until browned on the outside but still slightly pink in the centre. Add the garlic, chopped thyme and some seasoning and cook for 30 seconds.

3 Remove the pan from the heat, add the brandy and stir to release any flavoursome bits from the base of the pan.

4 Tip the contents of the pan into a food processor, add the cream cheese and process in short bursts until smooth. Press the mixture through a sieve, then taste and adjust the seasoning if necessary. Divide the pâté between four ramekins, garnish each with a sprig of thyme, cover and chill for at least 2 hours before serving.

**Top tip** Sieving the pâté mixture gives it a smooth and creamy texture without adding extra Points.

## CHARGRILLED CHICKEN CAESAR SALAD

**9 Points per recipe**

Serves 2

Preparation and cooking time:
15 minutes

Calories per serving: 276

Freezing: not recommended

A modern classic, this low Point version comes complete with a creamy dressing and crisp crunchy croutons.

25 g (1 oz) white bread, without crusts, cut into 1 cm (½ inch) dice
low fat cooking spray
2 × 125 g (4½ oz) skinless, boneless chicken breasts
2 tablespoons low fat mayonnaise
2 tablespoons low fat plain yogurt
½ teaspoon Dijon mustard
1 teaspoon lemon juice
3 tablespoons skimmed milk
1 small Cos lettuce, shredded roughly
10 g freshly grated Parmesan cheese
4 anchovy fillets, chopped finely
salt and freshly ground black pepper

**1** Preheat the oven to Gas Mark 4/ 180°C/fan oven 160°C.
**2** Spread out the diced bread on a baking tray and lightly coat with low fat cooking spray. Bake for 6–7 minutes until golden brown and crisp
**3** Meanwhile, preheat a griddle pan or non-stick frying pan on the hob. Cut each chicken breast in half horizontally to give two thin slices. Season and spray with low fat cooking spray then cook for 3–4 minutes each side or until cooked through.
**4** To make the dressing, whisk the mayonnaise, yogurt, mustard and lemon juice together with some seasoning and then gradually blend in the milk.
**5** Toss the shredded lettuce with half of the dressing then divide between two plates or bowls. Scatter the Parmesan, anchovies and croutons over the salads then top with the cooked chicken, sliced into thin strips, and drizzle with the remaining dressing. Serve immediately.

**Top tip** You can make double the quantity of croutons and store them in an airtight container to keep them crisp – they make a great low Point garnish for a bowl of soup.

**Variation** If you like garlic croutons, rub the bread with half a clove of garlic before cutting it into dice. The Points will remain the same.

## STEAK AU POIVRE WITH OVEN SAUTÉED POTATOES

**13 Points per recipe**

Serves 2

Preparation and cooking time:
30 minutes

Calories per serving: 418

Freezing: not recommended

These crispy oven sautéed potatoes are a delicious low Point alternative to chips – perfect with a juicy steak. Serve with fine green beans for a traditional French accompaniment.

**For the oven sautéed potatoes**
400 g (14 oz) potatoes, peeled and diced
low fat cooking spray
1 tablespoon chopped fresh rosemary
a pinch of coarse sea salt

**For the steak au poivre**
2 × 175 g (6 oz) rump steaks
½ teaspoon black peppercorns, crushed coarsely
low fat cooking spray
2 shallots, chopped finely
100 ml (3½ fl oz) red wine
100 ml (3½ fl oz) beef stock
salt

**1** Preheat the oven to Gas Mark 6/ 200°C/fan oven 180°C.
**2** Cook the potatoes in salted boiling water for 5 minutes and then drain well. Shake around in the pan to roughen the edges slightly then spread them out on a baking tray and lightly coat with low fat cooking spray. Roast for 20 minutes until golden and crisp.
**3** Meanwhile, press the peppercorns into the steaks and season with a little salt. Place a non-stick frying pan on the hob to preheat. When it is really hot, spray with low fat cooking spray and add the steaks. Sprinkle the shallots around the steaks. Cook the steaks for 2 minutes on each side for medium rare, or 3 minutes on each side for well done.
**4** Two minutes before the end of the cooking time add the wine and stock to the pan and allow it to boil until reduced and slightly syrupy.
**5** Toss the potatoes with the rosemary and some coarse sea salt and serve with the steaks and sauce.

**Top tip** Part cooking the potatoes and shaking them in the pan to roughen the edges before roasting helps to give a really crispy result. The same trick works well for roast potatoes.

## MEDITERRANEAN STUFFED PEPPERS

**8 Points per recipe**

 Serves 2

Preparation time: 10 minutes

Cooking time: 30 minutes

Calories per serving: 281

Freezing: not recommended

These colourful stuffed peppers make a superb supper dish, ideal served with a No Point mixed leaf salad. If you're cooking for one, keep the second portion for a deliciously different lunchbox solution, as they taste just as good cold.

1 red and 1 yellow pepper, halved through the stalk and deseeded

low fat cooking spray

50 g (1³/₄ oz) couscous

100 ml (3¹/₂ fl oz) hot vegetable stock

4 spring onions, sliced

15 g (¹/₂ oz) pine nuts

8 cherry tomatoes, quartered

1 tablespoon fresh chopped parsley

10 black olives, stoned and chopped

40g (1¹/₂ oz) feta cheese, diced

salt and freshly ground black pepper

1 Preheat the oven to Gas Mark 6/200°C/fan oven 180°C. Place the peppers in a roasting tin, cut side up, spray with low fat cooking spray and roast for 15 minutes.

2 Place the couscous in a bowl and pour in the hot stock. Cover the bowl with a plate and leave to stand for 5 minutes.

3 Heat a non-stick frying pan and spray with low fat cooking spray. Stir fry the spring onions and pine nuts for 3 minutes until lightly browned. Mix into the couscous, adding the remaining ingredients. Season well.

4 Stuff the peppers with the couscous mixture and return to the oven for 5 minutes. Serve one red and one yellow pepper half per person.

## CREAMY GARLIC CHICKEN WITH ROASTED TOMATOES

**8¹/₂ Points per recipe**

Serves 2

Preparation time: 5 minutes

Cooking time: 20 minutes

Calories per serving: 295

Freezing: not recommended

A luxurious recipe that is very quick to prepare, making it ideal for a special occasion. Serve with fine green beans and 100 g (3¹/₂ oz) new potatoes for 1 extra Point.

2 medium (165 g) skinless, boneless chicken breasts

40 g (1¹/₂ oz) Boursin light cheese

2 slices Parma ham

low fat cooking spray

175 g (6 oz) small tomatoes on the vine

1 teaspoon fresh thyme leaves

2 tablespoons balsamic vinegar

salt and freshly ground black pepper

1 Preheat the oven to Gas Mark 6/200°C/fan oven 180°C.

2 Cut a pocket in the side of each chicken breast and stuff with the Boursin cheese.

3 Season with salt and freshly ground black pepper, then wrap a slice of Parma ham around each one. Place in a roasting tin and spray with low fat cooking spray. Roast for 10 minutes.

4 Remove the tin from the oven, add the tomatoes on the vine and spray them with low fat cooking spray. Sprinkle the tomatoes with thyme and seasoning and drizzle with 1 tablespoon of balsamic vinegar. Roast for a further 8 minutes.

5 Lift the chicken and tomatoes out onto warmed plates, leaving behind any cheese that has oozed out. Add the remaining balsamic vinegar and 1 tablespoon of water to the tin. Place on a medium heat and whisk for 30 seconds to form a sauce. Pour over the chicken and serve.

**Creamy Garlic Chicken with Roasted Tomatoes:** Simply delicious and just 4 Points per serving.

## SAUSAGES IN CIDER WITH COLCANNON

**26½ Points per recipe**

Serves 4
Preparation time: 20 minutes
Cooking time: 30 minutes
Calories per serving: 503
Freezing: recommended (for sausages in cider only)

A wonderful family style casserole served with Colcannon, an Irish dish of mashed potatoes mixed with buttered cabbage. Delicious!

| |
|---|
| low fat cooking spray |
| 8 thick low fat sausages |
| 1 teaspoon olive oil |
| 1 large onion, sliced thickly |
| 150 g (5½ oz) turkey breast steak |
| 2 garlic cloves, crushed |
| 1 tablespoon chopped fresh thyme |
| 150 g (5½ oz) button mushrooms |
| 25 g (1 oz) plain flour |
| 300 ml (½ pint) dry cider |
| 150 ml (¼ pint) chicken stock |
| 1 tablespoon cider vinegar |
| salt and freshly ground black pepper |

**For the Colcannon**

| |
|---|
| 850 g (1 lb 14 oz) potatoes, peeled and cut into chunks |
| 100 ml (3½ fl oz) skimmed milk |
| 2 teaspoons half fat butter |
| ¼ Savoy cabbage, shredded |

1 Spray a non-stick frying pan with low fat cooking spray and heat, then brown the sausages all over.
2 Meanwhile, heat the olive oil in a flameproof casserole, add the onion and cook for 5 minutes until browned. Add the turkey strips, garlic, thyme and mushrooms and cook for 1 minute more. Stir in the flour, then gradually blend in the cider, stock and cider vinegar, and finally add the browned sausages. Bring to the boil, add seasoning, cover and simmer for 30 minutes.
3 Cook the potatoes in boiling salted water for 20 minutes or until tender. Drain into a colander. Heat the milk in the pan, then mash the potatoes into the milk. Cover and keep warm.
4 Melt the half fat butter in a pan with 4 tablespoons of water. Stir in the cabbage, cover and cook for 5 minutes. Stir the cabbage into the mashed potato, adding seasoning to taste. Serve with the braised sausages and gravy.

**Variation** You can use four turkey rashers, chopped roughly, instead of the turkey breast. The Points per serving will remain the same.

## TARTE TATIN

**20 Points per recipe**

 Serves 6
Preparation time: 20 minutes + 30 minutes chilling
Cooking time: 35 minutes
Calories per serving: 215
Freezing: not recommended

The French Tatin sisters allegedly invented this upside down dessert, when they dropped a tart as it came out of the oven!

**For the pastry**

| |
|---|
| 125 g (4½ oz) plain flour, plus 1 teaspoon to dust |
| pinch salt |
| 60 g (2 oz) polyunsaturated margarine |

**For the tarte**

| |
|---|
| 25 g (1 oz) polyunsaturated margarine |
| 25 g (1 oz) light brown soft sugar |
| 3 medium dessert apples |

1 Sift the flour and a pinch of salt into a bowl. Rub in the polyunsaturated margarine until the mixture resembles breadcrumbs. Add just enough cold water to bring the dough together. Shape into a disc, wrap in cling film and chill for 30 minutes.
2 Preheat the oven to Gas Mark 5/ 190°C/fan oven 170°C.
3 Blend the margarine and brown sugar together and spread over the base of a 24 cm (9½ inches) metal pie plate.
4 Cut each apple into 6 wedges and remove the cores. Arrange in the pie plate, in a circular pattern. Cut any extra wedges into small pieces and fit into the gaps.
5 Roll out the pastry on a floured work surface to a disc slightly larger than the pie dish. Lift the pastry on top of the apples and tuck the edges down the side of the dish. Place on a baking tray and bake for 20–25 minutes until the pastry is crisp and golden.
6 Leave to cool for 10 minutes while you preheat the grill. Turn the tarte tatin out onto the baking tray and grill for 2–3 minutes until lightly caramelised. Serve warm.

**Top tip** Use a pleasantly sharp eating apple, such as a Cox or Braeburn for the best flavour in this recipe.

Sausages in Cider with Colcannon: The ultimate comfort food for just 6½ Points per serving.

4  Pour the caramel into a 20 cm (8 inch) diameter soufflé dish and swirl around to coat the base and sides of the dish. Leave to set.

5  Add the milk and the remaining sugar to the caramel saucepan. Heat to simmering point, stirring to dissolve any caramel in the pan. Whisk the eggs and vanilla in a mixing bowl, and then gradually pour the hot milk over the eggs. Strain into the caramel coated soufflé dish through a sieve, to remove any egg threads.

6  Place the dish in a roasting tin and fill the tin with hot water from the kettle. Bake in the oven for 45 minutes until the custard feels firm and set in the centre. Remove from the hot water, leave to cool, then chill, covered, for at least 2 hours before serving.

7  Run a palette knife around the edge of the dish and turn out onto a lipped dish to hold the sauce.

**Top tips** Take care when making caramel, as boiling sugar can cause nasty burns. If there is any caramel left stuck to the pan, add hot water and bring to the boil to dissolve it.

The crème caramel is cooked in a bath of hot water (known as a bain marie) to prevent the mixture getting too hot and curdling. This method ensures a smooth, silky texture.

**Variation** You can make individual crème caramels in six 150 ml (¼ pint) ramekins.

**Crème Caramel: Enjoy this French classic for just 2½ Points per serving.**

## CRÈME CARAMEL

technique, this classic French dessert is sure to become a firm favourite.

**15 Points per recipe**

Ⓥ  *Serves 6*

*Preparation time: 15 minutes*

*Cooking time: 45 minutes + 2 hours chilling*

*Calories per serving: 186*

*Freezing: not recommended*

Many people worry about making caramel, but if you follow the instructions you'll find that it's really very simple – it's just a case of having the patience to let the sugar dissolve completely, and then cooking it to the required toffee colour. Once you've mastered the

*140 g (5 oz) granulated sugar*

*600 ml (1 pt) skimmed milk*

*4 eggs, beaten*

*1 teaspoon vanilla extract*

1  Preheat the oven to Gas Mark 2/ 150°C/fan oven 130°C.

2  Place 110 g (4 oz) granulated sugar in a non-stick pan with 4 tablespoons of boiling water and stir over a gentle heat until the sugar has completely dissolved.

3  Increase the heat and boil the syrup until it reaches a rich golden brown colour, which will take around 5 minutes.

# SUMMER FRUIT PROFITEROLES

**19 Points per recipe**

*Serves 6*

*Makes 18 profiteroles*

*Preparation time: 20 minutes + cooling*

*Cooking time: 25 minutes*

*Calories per serving: 197*

*Freezing: not recommended*

**For the profiteroles**

75 g (2³⁄₄ oz) plain flour

salt

60 g (2 oz) polyunsaturated margarine

2 eggs, beaten

**For the sauce**

250 g (9 oz) frozen summer fruits, defrosted

1¹⁄₂ tablespoons granulated sweetener

**For the filling**

250 g (9 oz) Quark

1 teaspoon vanilla extract

2 tablespoons granulated sweetener

**1** Preheat the oven to Gas Mark 6/ 200°C/fan oven 180°C.

**2** Sift the flour and a pinch of salt onto a piece of greaseproof paper that has been folded in half and then opened out again.

**3** Place the margarine in a non-stick saucepan with 150 ml (5 fl oz) cold water and bring to the boil. Remove from the heat and tip in the flour, stirring with a wooden spoon until the mixture comes together in a smooth ball. Sit the pan in a basin of cold water until the dough is cool.

**4** Gradually beat in the eggs, until you have a smooth batter that drops easily from the spoon. Scatter droplets of water over two baking sheets, then place 9 heaped teaspoonfuls of the batter onto each tray, leaving room for the profiteroles to rise.

**5** Bake for 18–20 minutes until the profiteroles are well risen and quite brown. Make a small hole in each one to release the steam then return to the oven for a further 5 minutes to crisp up. Cool on a wire rack.

**6** Blend the berries to a purée in a food processor or liquidizer, then pass through a sieve to remove any pips and seeds. Stir in the granulated sweetener.

**7** Mix the Quark, vanilla extract and sweetener together. Split the profiteroles open and stuff each one with a teaspoon of filling. Serve three profiteroles per person, with the sauce poured over the top.

***Top tips*** Don't fill the profiteroles too far in advance (30 minutes at the most) as they will start to go soft.

The creamy filling for these light and squidgy profiteroles is based on Quark, a low fat curd cheese with a smooth texture and slightly tangy flavour that can be used in both sweet and savoury recipes. It is available from the dairy chiller cabinet in most supermarkets.

**Summer Fruit Profiteroles: With a delicious creamy filling, these are a wonderful treat at 3 Points per serving.**

# pub grub

This is great British food at its glorious best – perfectly suited to the whole family's needs. With generous portions of hearty fare, these recipes are low Point versions of real traditional favourites, from a creamy vegetable soup and prawn cocktail right through to casseroles and yummy stodgy puddings!

## CHICKEN AND MUSHROOM PIE

**24½ Points per recipe**

*Serves 4*

*Preparation time: 25 minutes +*
*30 minutes chilling*

*Cooking time: 25 minutes*

*Calories per serving: 380*

*Freezing: recommended*

Serve this richly flavoured pie with a colourful mixture of carrots, broccoli and cauliflower, adding 100g (3½ oz) boiled new potatoes for an extra 1 Point per person if you are feeling really hungry.

**For the pastry**

*150 g (5½ oz) plain flour*

*pinch salt*

*65 g (2¼ oz) polyunsaturated margarine*

**For the filling**

*low fat cooking spray*

*2 medium skinless, boneless chicken breasts, diced*

*1 medium onion, sliced thinly*

*2 garlic cloves, crushed*

*250 g (9 oz) closed cup mushrooms, quartered*

*1 heaped tablespoon plain flour*

*1 tablespoon chopped fresh sage or 1 teaspoon dried sage*

*10 g porcini, snipped into small pieces*

*100 ml (3½ fl oz) white wine*

*300 ml (½ pint) chicken stock*

*1 tablespoon skimmed milk, to brush*

*salt and freshly ground black pepper*

**1** Sift the flour and a pinch of salt into a bowl. Rub in the polyunsaturated margarine until the mixture resembles breadcrumbs. Add just enough cold water to bring the dough together. Shape into a disc, wrap in cling film and chill for 30 minutes.

**2** Preheat the oven to Gas Mark 5/ 190°C/fan oven 170°C.

**3** Heat a non-stick frying pan on the hob, spray with low fat cooking spray and then brown the chicken pieces in two batches. Remove the chicken onto a plate.

**4** In the frying pan, soften the onion for 3 minutes before adding the garlic and fresh mushrooms. Cook for 2 minutes more. Stir in the flour, sage and porcini, then gradually blend in the wine and chicken stock. Return the chicken to the pan. Bring to the boil, season, then cover and simmer for 15 minutes. Tip into a ceramic pie dish with a lip and cool for 10 minutes.

**5** Roll out the pastry to a circle slightly larger than the top of the dish. Cut a narrow strip of pastry from around the outside, brush the edge of the dish with water and press the pastry stirp onto the lip of the dish. Dampen the pastry border, then lift the pastry lid into place. Press down well and trim the edges. Use a fork to stamp a pattern around the edge, and use the pastry trimmings to decorate the top. Brush with the milk and then bake the pie for 25 minutes until crisp and golden.

**Top tip** Porcini are Italian dried mushrooms that give a wonderfully concentrated flavour to this recipe.

**Chicken and Mushroom Pie:** Enjoy a generous portion of this delicious pie for just 6 Points.

Deluxe Prawn Cocktail: A traditional favourite with a modern twist for just 2 Points per serving.

## DELUXE PRAWN COCKTAIL

**8 Points per recipe**

*Serves 4*

*Preparation and cooking time:*
*10 minutes*

*Calories per serving: 126*

*Freezing: not recommended*

White crabmeat, rocket and asparagus give this traditional favourite an upmarket new twist.

| |
|---|
| ¼ Iceberg lettuce, shredded |
| 25 g (1 oz) rocket leaves |
| 100 g ( 3½ oz) asparagus tips, halved |
| 12 cherry tomatoes, quartered |
| 175 g (6 oz) small prawns, defrosted |
| 170g can white crabmeat, drained |
| cayenne pepper |

**For the cocktail sauce**

| |
|---|
| 2 tablespoons low fat mayonnaise |
| 2 tablespoons low fat plain yogurt |
| 2 tablespoons tomato ketchup |
| ½ tablespoon lime juice |
| 2 tablespoons skimmed milk |
| salt and freshly ground black pepper |

**1** Toss the Iceberg lettuce and rocket together and divide between four glass dishes or plates. Cook the asparagus in salted boiling water for 3 minutes, then drain and refresh under a cold tap. Scatter the asparagus tips and cherry tomatoes over the salad. Divide the prawns and crabmeat between the dishes.

**2** Mix the mayonnaise, yogurt, ketchup and lime juice together with some seasoning in a small bowl, then gradually whisk in the milk until smooth.

**3** Drizzle the sauce over each dish just before serving and add a dusting of the cayenne pepper.

## CREAMY VEGETABLE SOUP

**1 Points per recipe**

Ⓥ *Serves 6*

*Preparation time: 15 minutes*

*Cooking time: 20 minutes*

*Calories per serving: 124*

*Freezing: recommended*

Butternut squash gives this No Point soup a wonderfully creamy, velvety texture. Serve swirled with a tablespoon of low fat plain yogurt and a few snipped chives for an extra ½ Point.

| |
|---|
| low fat cooking spray |
| 3 medium leeks, trimmed, washed and sliced |
| 3 large carrots, peeled and diced |
| 1 medium butternut squash, peeled, deseeded and diced |
| 1 litre (1¾ pints) hot vegetable stock |
| 300 ml (½ pint) skimmed milk |
| juice of ½ lemon |
| salt and freshly ground black pepper |

**1** Spray a large saucepan with low fat cooking spray, add the leeks, cover and cook over a medium heat for 4 minutes until softened.

**2** Add the remaining ingredients and bring to the boil. Cover with a lid, leaving it slightly ajar, and simmer for 20 minutes until the vegetables are tender.

**3** Liquidise the soup in batches and adjust the seasoning to taste.

***Top tip*** If you find butternut squash difficult to peel, invest in a 'U' shaped peeler – it makes life much easier, and will only cost a couple of pounds.

## GAMMON AND SPICED PINEAPPLE

**12½ Points per recipe**

*Serves 2*

*Preparation and cooking time:*
*10 minutes*

*Calories per serving: 316*

*Freezing: not recommended*

A slightly spicy sweet and sour sauce lends a twist to this old favourite. Serve with some broccoli and 100 g (3½ oz) boiled new potatoes for an extra 1 Point per serving.

| |
|---|
| 2 × 150 g (5½ oz) gammon plate steaks |
| 220 g can sliced pineapples in juice |
| ¼ teaspoon ground mixed spice |
| 1 tablespoon cider or white wine vinegar |
| 1 teaspoon cornflour |
| low fat cooking spray |

**1** Cook the gammon steaks for 8–10 minutes under a preheated grill, turning half way through cooking.

**2** Meanwhile, drain the juice from the pineapple into a jug and whisk in the mixed spice, vinegar and 3 tablespoons of water. In a small bowl, blend the cornflour with 1 tablespoon of water.

**3** Heat a non-stick frying pan on the hob. Pat the pineapple rings dry on kitchen paper, spray the pan with low fat cooking spray then fry the pineapple rings for 2 minutes on each side until caramelised.

**4** Pour the pineapple juice mixture into the frying pan and bubble for 30 seconds until slightly reduced. Add the blended cornflour and stir until thickened.

**5** Serve the gammon steaks on warmed plates, topped with the caramelised pineapple and sauce.

## BEEF IN BEER WITH MUSTARD AND THYME DUMPLINGS

**26 Points per recipe**

Serves 4

Preparation time: 25 minutes

Cooking time: 1 hour 45 minutes

Calories per serving: 485

Freezing: recommended (for beef in beer only)

Melt in the mouth dumplings top this hearty casserole – all you need to go with it is a big bowl of No Point green cabbage.

400 g (14 oz) lean casserole beef steak, cubed

low fat cooking spray

1 onion, cut into wedges

2 celery sticks, chopped

2 leeks, cut into chunks

3 carrots, peeled and cut into chunks

1 heaped tablespoon plain flour

300 ml (½ pint) beer or ale

600 ml (1 pint) beef stock

175 g (6 oz) mushrooms, sliced thickly

salt and freshly ground black pepper

**For the dumplings**

110 g (4 oz) self raising flour

½ teaspoon baking powder

salt

½ tablespoon chopped fresh thyme leaves

1 tablespoon whole grain mustard

50 g (1¾ oz) polyunsaturated margarine

1 Dry fry the meat in batches in a non-stick frying pan, removing the meat onto a plate when it is well browned all over. Preheat the oven to Gas Mark 2/150°C/fan oven 130°C.

2 Heat the low fat cooking spray in an ovenproof casserole, add the onion wedges and brown well on both sides.

3 Heat the low fat cooking spray in a frying pan, add the celery, leeks and carrots and cook for 2 minutes until lightly browned. Stir in the flour then gradually blend in the beer or ale and beef stock. Pour everything into the casserole, then add the browned meat. Season and stir well, then bring the sauce to a simmer. Cover the casserole with a tight fitting lid and transfer to the oven to cook for 1 hour 15 minutes.

4 To make the dumplings, sift the flour, baking powder and a pinch of salt into a mixing bowl. Stir in the thyme and mustard, then rub in the margarine until the mixture resembles breadcrumbs. Add just enough cold water to bring the mixture together as a soft dough. Shape into eight dumplings.

5 Remove the casserole from the oven, stir the mushrooms into the sauce then arrange the dumplings on top. Replace the lid, return to the oven and cook for 30 minutes.

## FISH AND CHIPS

**24 Points per recipe**

Serves 4

Preparation time: 10 minutes

Cooking time: 20 minutes

Calories per serving: 415

Freezing: not recommended

Take away chips might be delicious, but they are very high in Points. With these scrumptious homemade chips, you get a generously sized portion for only 3½ Points per person. So now you can enjoy fish and chips and still lose weight!

**For the chips**

900 g (2lb) potatoes, peeled

1 vegetable stock cube

1½ tablespoons vegetable oil

**For the fish**

1 egg, beaten

2 tablespoons skimmed milk

75 g (2¾ oz) fresh white breadcrumbs

¼ teaspoon ground turmeric

4 × 150 g (5½ oz) haddock fillets

low fat cooking spray

salt and freshly ground black pepper

1 Preheat the oven to Gas Mark 6/200°C/fan oven 180°C.

2 Cut the potatoes into chips about 15mm (⅝ inch) across. Add the vegetable stock cube to a pan of boiling water and tip in the chips. Cover and cook for 5 minutes until just tender. Drain the chips into a colander.

3 Beat the egg with the milk and some seasoning then pour into a shallow dish. Mix the breadcrumbs and turmeric together and spread out on a plate. Pat the fish dry on kitchen paper then dip each piece first in the egg, then in breadcrumbs to coat. Place on a baking tray and spray lightly with low fat cooking spray.

4 Carefully toss the chips in the oil and spread them out on a large baking tray. Sprinkle with salt, then place on the top shelf of the oven. Cook for 5 minutes, then add the tray of fish to the oven and cook both for 15 minutes.

5 Serve up the fish and chips on to warmed serving plates.

# SPICY BEAN BURGERS

**17 Points per recipe**

 Serves 4

*Preparation time 20 minutes + 2 hours chilling*

*Cooking time: 10 minutes*

*Calories per serving: 293*

*Freezing: recommended (at the end of step 2)*

Tinned beans are a really good low Point source of protein for vegetarians. Combined with vegetables, spices and breadcrumbs, they make for a seriously filling veggie burger.

### For the bean burgers

low fat cooking spray

1 medium onion, finely chopped

2 garlic cloves, crushed

1 red chilli, deseeded and chopped

1 courgette, grated

410g can cannellini beans, rinsed and drained

1 egg white

grated zest ½ lemon

1 tablespoon chopped fresh parsley

½ teaspoon ground cumin

60 g (2 oz) fresh white breadcrumbs

1 tablespoon plain flour

salt and freshly ground black pepper

### To serve

4 burger buns

4 tablespoons tomato and chilli relish or tomato relish

few curly lettuce leaves

1 small red onion, sliced

1 large tomato, sliced

1  Heat the low fat cooking spray in a non-stick frying pan. Add the onion and cook for 3 minutes until golden, then add the garlic, chilli and courgette and stir-fry for 3 minutes until wilted. Set aside to cool slightly.

2  Tip the beans into a food processor, add the egg white, lemon zest, parsley and cumin and blend to a paste. Scrape into a mixing bowl, adding the courgette mixture, breadcrumbs and a generous amount of seasoning. Mix together thoroughly then shape into four burgers. Cover and chill for 2 hours to firm up.

3  Heat a non-stick frying pan on the hob. Dust the burgers with the flour, spray the pan with low fat cooking spray and fry the bean burgers for 4–5 minutes on each side.

4  Split and lightly toast the burger buns. Spread one half of each with a spoonful of relish, add some lettuce then top with a bean burger, sliced red onion and tomato. Top with the remaining half burger bun and serve at once.

**Spicy Bean Burgers: These will satisfy the heartiest of appetites for just 4 Points per serving.**

**Plum Cobbler:
A comforting
home-style
dessert for only
4½ Points per
serving.**

## PLUM COBBLER

**27½ Points per recipe**

Ⓥ Serves 6

*Preparation time: 15 minutes*

*Cooking time: 25 minutes*

*Calories per serving: 257*

*Freezing: not recommended*

A cobbler is a rustic scone-like topping that is used to top a hot fruity dessert, and makes a pleasant change from crumble. Serve with low fat custard or low fat vanilla ice cream, adding the extra Points.

*60 g (2 oz) demerara sugar*

*900 g (2 lb) plums, halved and stoned*

*½ teaspoon ground cinnamon*

**For the cobbler topping**

*125 ml (4 fl oz) skimmed milk*

*1 tablespoon lemon juice*

*175 g (6 oz) plain flour*

*1 teaspoon baking powder*

*salt*

*30 g (1¼ oz) caster sugar*

*30 g (1¼ oz) polyunsaturated margarine*

**1** Preheat the oven to Gas Mark 5/ 190°C/fan oven 170°C.

**2** Mix the lemon juice into the skimmed milk and leave to stand for 5 minutes, during which time the milk will curdle – this is normal.

**3** Reserve 1 tablespoon of demerara sugar for the topping, then place the remaining sugar in a pan with the plums, cinnamon and 125 ml (4 fl oz) water. Cover and simmer for 5 minutes then tip into a baking dish.

**4** Sift the flour, baking powder and a pinch of salt in to a mixing bowl. Stir in the caster sugar then rub in the margarine until the mixture looks like breadcrumbs. Using a round bladed knife, add the 'soured milk' to bind the cobbler mixture to a soft and slightly sticky dough.

**5** Dollop rough spoonfuls of the cobbler dough on top of the plums, then scatter with the reserved demerara sugar.

**6** Place on a baking tray and bake on the centre shelf of the oven for 25 minutes until the cobbler topping is golden brown and crusty. Leave to stand for 5 minutes before serving.

**Variation** To make a rhubarb cobbler, use 750 g (1 lb 10 oz) chopped rhubarb in place of the plums, increase the sugar to 75 g (2¾ oz) and flavour with ground ginger instead of cinnamon. This will be 4 Points per serving.

## TOFFEE BANANA PUDDINGS

**24½ Points per recipe**

Serves 8

*Preparation time: 20 minutes*

*Cooking time: 20 minutes*

*Calories per serving: 270*

*Freezing: recommended (for puddings only)*

If you need to look for an excuse to indulge in toffee pudding, this is a great way to use up those brown speckled bananas that are left in the fruit bowl!

*110 g (4 oz) stoned dates, chopped*

*2 ripe medium bananas, mashed*

*½ level teaspoon bicarbonate of soda*

*1 teaspoon vanilla extract*

*low fat cooking spray*

*50 g (1¾ oz) dark muscovado sugar*

*50 g (1¾ oz) polyunsaturated margarine*

*2 eggs, beaten*

*175 g (6 oz) self raising flour*

*salt*

**For the sauce**

*25 g (1 oz) dark muscovado sugar*

*200ml tub very low fat plain fromage frais*

*1 medium banana, sliced, to serve*

**1** Preheat the oven to Gas Mark 4/ 180°C/fan oven 160°C.

**2** Gently simmer the dates in 150 ml (5 fl oz) boiling water for 5 minutes until they have absorbed all the liquid. Tip into a bowl and stir in the mashed bananas, bicarbonate of soda and vanilla extract. Set aside to cool slightly.

**3** Lightly spray eight metal pudding basins with the low fat cooking spray and arrange on a baking tray.

**4** Cream the sugar and margarine together in a mixing bowl using an electric whisk, then gradually beat in the eggs. Stir in the banana date mixture, then sift in the flour and a pinch of salt. Fold the mixture together with a metal spoon until well combined. Divide the batter between the pudding basins then bake on the centre shelf for 15–20 minutes until risen and firm to the touch.

**5** For the toffee sauce, mix the sugar and fromage frais together in a bowl and set aside for 15 minutes to allow the sugar to dissolve into the sauce.

**6** When the puddings are ready, run a small palette knife around the edge of each pudding basin to loosen the sponge and turn it out onto a dessert plate. Top each sponge with a few slices of banana and serve drizzled with the toffee sauce.

# italian

Italian restaurant dishes often come laden with olive oil or cheese, which send the Points sky high. However, it doesn't mean you need to skip your favourite dishes, such as risotto, lasagne, pizza and tiramisu, as you'll find low Point versions of all these and more in this chapter.

## PASTA PUTTANESCA

**7 Points per recipe**

*Serves 2*

*Preparation and cooking time:*
*10 minutes*

*Calories per serving: 271*

*Freezing: not recommended*

Puttanesca is a deliciously spicy and rustic Italian sauce, full of gutsy flavours.

---

*125 g (4½ oz) dried penne*

*salt*

*low fat cooking spray*

*1 garlic clove, crushed*

*pinch crushed dried chillies*

*1 tablespoon torn fresh basil, plus extra to garnish*

*1 tablespoon capers, rinsed and drained*

*10 black olives, stoned and chopped*

*1 teaspoon tomato purée*

*4 anchovy fillets, chopped (optional)*

*230 g can chopped tomatoes*

**1** Cook the penne in boiling salted water according to the pack instructions.

---

**2** Spray a saucepan with low fat cooking spray, add the garlic and crushed chillies and cook for 30 seconds. Add the remaining ingredients and simmer the sauce for 5 minutes.

**3** Add 2 tablespoons of the pasta cooking water to the sauce, then toss with the drained penne. Serve in warmed bowls, garnished with fresh basil.

**Variation** For a vegetarian or vegan alternative, simply leave out the anchovies. The Points will then be 3 per serving.

**Pasta Puttanesca:
This is ideal for a
quick mid-week
supper at just 3½
Points per serving.**

## MINESTRONE SOUP

**4½ Points per recipe**

**V** **Vg** Serves 4

Preparation time: 15 minutes

Cooking time: 25 minutes

Calories per serving: 135

Freezing: not recommended

This rustic Italian soup is delicious served with 1 teaspoon grated Parmesan cheese sprinkled on top for an extra ½ Point. It's very filling, and makes an ideal supper.

| |
| --- |
| 2 teaspoons olive oil |
| 1 medium onion, chopped |
| 2 sticks celery, chopped |
| 2 carrots, peeled and diced |
| 2 garlic cloves, sliced |
| 230 g can chopped tomatoes |
| 1 tablespoon tomato purée |
| 2 tablespoons chopped fresh basil |
| 1.2 litres (2 pints) vegetable stock |
| 1 courgette, diced |
| 75 g (2¾ oz) green cabbage, shredded finely |
| 60 g (2 oz) mini pasta shapes |
| salt and freshly ground black pepper |

**1** Heat the oil in a large saucepan, add the onion and cook for 3 minutes, then stir in the celery, carrots and garlic, cover and cook gently for 5 minutes.

**2** Stir in the chopped tomatoes, tomato purée, basil, stock and seasoning. Bring to the boil, cover and simmer for 15 minutes.

**3** Add the courgette, cabbage and pasta, re-cover the pan and simmer for 10 minutes. Serve immediately.

***Top tip*** If you don't have mini pasta shapes in your storecupboard, use the same weight of spaghetti, broken into short lengths.

## SPINACH AND FOUR CHEESE CANNELLONI

**31½ Points per recipe**

**V** (if using vegetarian cheese)

Serves 6

Preparation time: 25 minutes

Cooking time: 25 minutes

Calories per serving: 285

Freezing: recommended

It's hard to believe for a dish so low in Points, but these baked cannelloni really do contain four cheeses: ricotta, Quark, Parmesan and mozzarella. Serve with a No Point tomato and basil salad, drizzled with a little balsamic vinegar.

| |
| --- |
| low fat cooking spray |
| 1 medium onion, chopped finely |
| 2 garlic cloves, crushed |
| 225 g (8 oz) frozen spinach |
| 150 g (5½ oz) ricotta cheese |
| 250 g (9 oz) Quark |
| 25 g (1 oz) freshly grated Parmesan cheese |
| freshly grated nutmeg |
| 18 cannelloni tubes |
| 700 g jar passata |
| 125 g (4½ oz) light mozzarella cheese, drained and diced |
| 1 tablespoon shredded basil |
| salt and freshly ground black pepper |
| fresh basil leaves, to serve |

**1** Preheat the oven to Gas Mark 5/190°C/fan oven 170°C.

**2** Heat the low fat cooking spray in a saucepan, add the onion and cook for 5 minutes until softened. Add the garlic and spinach, cover the pan and cook for 5 minutes, stirring occasionally, until the spinach is defrosted. Tip into a bowl and leave to cool slightly.

**3** Stir in the ricotta, Quark and half the Parmesan, add the nutmeg and seasoning to taste then use this mixture to stuff the cannelloni tubes.

**4** Pour a quarter of the passata over the base of an ovenproof dish. Tuck the filled cannelloni into the dish and scatter the mozzarella over the top. Pour the remaining passata over the cannelloni, then add the basil and remaining Parmesan. Bake for 25 minutes until bubbling hot. Serve three cannelloni per person, garnished with fresh basil leaves.

***Top tip*** The easiest way to fill the cannelloni is to use a piping bag, minus the nozzle. If you don't have one, improvise with a large plastic food bag: place the filling inside and fold over the top several times to close, then snip off a sealed corner and squeeze the filling into the cannelloni tubes.

**Spinach and Four Cheese Cannelloni: Cheesy and satisfying and only 5 Points.**

### GNOCCHI WITH A NO POINT TOMATO AND BASIL SAUCE

**6½ Points per recipe**

Ⓥ Serves 2

*Preparation and cooking time:*
*10 minutes*

*Calories per serving: 278*

*Freezing: not recommended*

Gnocchi are little Italian potato dumplings; a great store cupboard standby that are seriously filling.

---

*low fat cooking spray*

*1 large courgette, diced*

*1 small garlic clove, crushed*

*1 tablespoon chopped fresh basil, plus extra to garnish*

*230 g can chopped tomatoes*

*6 cherry tomatoes, halved*

*300 g (10½ oz) gnocchi*

*½ teaspoon granulated sweetener*

*salt and freshly ground black pepper*

---

**1** Spray a non stick saucepan with low fat cooking spray, add the diced courgette and stir fry over a high heat for 3 minutes until beginning to brown.

**2** Add the garlic, basil, tinned and cherry tomatoes, plus some seasoning. Bring the sauce to the boil and simmer briskly for 5 minutes.

**3** Bring a large pan of salted water to the boil, add the gnocchi and cook for 2–3 minutes: they are ready when they start to float to the surface. Drain the gnocchi and tip into warmed bowls.

**4** Stir the sweetener into the sauce then ladle it over the hot gnocchi. Garnish with fresh basil.

**Top tip** Adding sweetener counteracts the acidity of canned tomatoes and gives a fuller, rounder flavour.

### MUSHROOM RISOTTO

**9½ Points per recipe**

Ⓥ Serves 2

*Preparation time: 10 minutes*

*Cooking time: 25 minutes*

*Calories per serving: 332*

*Freezing: not recommended*

Italian risotto rice swells up as it cooks, so you only need a small portion of dried rice to create a generous bowlful of finished risotto. Serve with a No Point mixed salad.

---

*2 teaspoons polyunsaturated margarine*

*1 small onion, chopped finely*

*250 g (9 oz) closed cup mushrooms, chopped*

*5 g porcini, snipped*

*100 g (3½ oz) Italian risotto rice*

*100 ml (3½ fl oz) dry white wine*

*450 ml (16 fl oz) hot vegetable stock*

*15 g (½ oz) freshly grated Parmesan cheese*

*salt and freshly ground black pepper*

---

**1** Melt the margarine in a saucepan, add the onion and soften for 3 minutes. Add the fresh mushrooms and the porcini and cook for 3 minutes then stir in the rice and wine.

**2** Keep the vegetable stock hot in a pan over a low heat. Add a third of the stock to the rice and leave to bubble gently until it has been absorbed, stirring occasionally. Repeat with the remaining stock, in two batches, until the rice has absorbed it all and is tender, which should take 20–25 minutes. If the rice isn't quite cooked at this stage, add a little hot water and cook for 5 minutes more.

**3** Season, and stir in half the Parmesan. Serve in warmed bowls, sprinkled with the remaining Parmesan.

### SPAGHETTI CARBONARA

**10½ Points per recipe**

Serves 2

*Preparation and cooking time:*
*12 minutes*

*Calories per serving: 335*

*Freezing: not recommended*

This low Point version of a luscious Italian classic just goes to show that you really can eat anything you like with *Time To Eat*.

---

*125 g (4½ oz) dried quick cook spaghetti*

*1 egg*

*1 tablespoon half fat crème fraiche*

*1 teaspoon freshly grated Parmesan*

*low fat cooking spray*

*3 turkey rashers, cut into strips*

*salt and freshly ground black pepper*

---

**1** Bring a large pan of salted water to the boil. Add the spaghetti and cook for 12 minutes or according to pack instructions.

**2** Beat the egg, crème fraiche and Parmesan together with some seasoning.

**3** Fry the turkey rasher strips in low fat cooking spray for 1 minute in a non-stick pan.

**4** Drain the spaghetti and return to the warm pan. Add the egg mixture and hot turkey rashers, tossing together well to coat in the sauce. The egg will cling to the spaghetti and be lightly cooked by the heat of the pasta, but the sauce should remain creamy. Serve straightway.

**Variation** For a vegetarian version, use 110 g (4 oz) sliced mushrooms in place of the turkey rashers. The Points per serving will be 4½ .

Spaghetti
Carbonara:
An Italian
favourite for
an unbelievable
5½ Points!

**Pizza Calzone:**
**Enjoy this "pizza**
**pie" stuffed with**
**colourful layers**
**of soft cheese**
**and pimientos in**
**tomato sauce –**
**all for 6 Points.**

## PIZZA CALZONE

**6 POINTS**

A calzone is a pizza that has been folded over to enclose the filling – rather like a giant Cornish pasty. If you've never tried making pizza dough before, do give it a go as it really is very simple, plus the kneading is a great way of working out any built up tension! Serve with a crisp No Point mixed salad.

**12 Points per recipe**

Ⓥ *Serves 2*

*Preparation time: 20 minutes plus*
*1 hour rising*
*Cooking time: 15 minutes*
*Calories per serving: 399*
*Freezing: not recommended*

**For the pizza dough**

*175 g (6 oz) plain flour, plus extra for kneading*

*1 teaspoon fast action yeast*

*½ teaspoon sugar*

*1 teaspoon olive oil*

*salt and freshly ground black pepper*

**For the filling**

*100 g (3½ oz) Quark*

*2 teaspoons freshly grated Parmesan cheese*

*75 g (2¾ oz) pimientos preserved in brine, drained and sliced*

*1 tablespoon shredded fresh basil*

*3 tablespoons passata*

**1** Sift the flour into a mixing bowl, then stir in the yeast, sugar and ½ teaspoon salt. Make a well in the centre, pour in the oil and add enough warm water to bring the dough together – about 125 ml (4 fl oz).

**2** Turn out onto a floured surface and knead for 3 minutes until smooth. Return to the bowl, cover with clingfilm and leave to rise for 1 hour, or until doubled in bulk.

**3** Preheat the oven to gas Mark 6/ 200°C/fan oven 180°C.

**4** For the filling, mix the Quark and Parmesan together with some seasoning. Mix the pimientos, basil and passata together.

**5** Divide the dough ball in half and roll each out to an 18 cm (7 inches) circle. Transfer to a baking sheet.

**6** Spread the Quark mixture over half of each dough circle and top this with the pimento mixture. Moisten the edges with water, fold the untopped dough over the filling and pinch the edges to seal. Make a small hole in the top of each Calzone.

**7** Bake for 10–12 minutes until crisp and golden.

**Top tips** Make double the quantity of pizza dough and roll out a 25 cm (10 inch) pizza base. To make pizza marinara open freeze on a baking tray until firm then wrap well (in clingfilm). Top and cook the base from frozen, adding an extra 3 minutes to the cooking time.

**Variation** For a meaty Calzone, substitute dry-fried mushrooms, cooked spinach and 60 g (2 oz) wafer thin ham for the Quark, Parmesan and pimientos. The Points per serving will then be 5.

## TRADITIONAL LASAGNE

**37½ Points per recipe**

Serves 6

Preparation time: 30 minutes

Cooking time: 1 hour 25 minutes

Calories per serving: 382

Freezing: recommended

A homemade lasagne beats a bought version hands down every time.

9 sheets no pre-cook lasagne

25 g (1 oz) freshly grated Parmesan

**For the meat sauce**

500 g (1lb 2 oz) extra lean minced beef

1 tablespoon olive oil

1 large onion, chopped

2 garlic cloves, crushed

1 large carrot, peeled and grated

1 courgette, grated

400 g can chopped tomatoes

4 tablespoons tomato purée

100 ml (3½ fl oz) red wine

300 ml (10 fl oz) beef stock

salt and freshly ground black pepper

**For the white sauce**

40 g (1½ oz) sauce flour (see tip)

600 ml (1 pt) skimmed milk

2 bay leaves

**1** Brown the mince in two batches in a non-stick frying pan, then transfer to a flameproof casserole dish.

**2** Heat the oil in the frying pan, add the onion and soften for 3 minutes. Stir in the garlic, carrot and courgette and stir fry for 3 minutes, then add to the casserole. Stir in the remaining meat sauce ingredients and seasoning then bring to a simmer. Cover and cook gently for 45 minutes.

**3** To make the white sauce, blend the sauce flour with 2 tablespoons of the milk in a saucepan, then whisk in the remaining milk. Add the bay leaves and seasoning, then bring the sauce to the boil, stirring continuously until thickened and smooth. Simmer for 3 minutes. Remove from the heat and discard the bay leaves. Press cling film over the surface of the sauce to stop a skin forming, and set aside.

**4** Preheat the oven to Gas Mark 4/ 180°C/fan oven 160°C. Spoon a quarter of the meat sauce into the base of an ovenproof dish, cover with 3 lasagne sheets and another layer of meat sauce. Repeat the layers of lasagne and meat sauce twice more then pour the white sauce all over the top. Sprinkle with the Parmesan then bake for 40 minutes until golden brown.

**Top tip** If you can't find sauce flour, use 3 tablespoons of cornflour instead. The Points per serving will remain the same.

## PIZZA MARINARA

**14½ Points per recipe**

Serves 2

Preparation time: 20 minutes plus 1 hour rising

Cooking time: 12 minutes

Calories per serving: 518

Freezing: not recommended

This seafood topped pizza goes perfectly with a No Point mixed leaf salad with a lemony dressing.

**For the pizza dough**

150 g (5½ oz) plain flour, plus 1 tbsp for kneading

1 teaspoon fast-action yeast

½ teaspoon sugar

1 teaspoon olive oil

salt

**For the topping**

230 g can chopped tomatoes

1 garlic clove, crushed

100 g (3½ oz) asparagus tips

½ red pepper, thinly sliced

125 g (4½ oz) prawns, defrosted if necessary

50 g (1¾ oz) light mozzarella cheese, diced

**1** Sift the flour into a mixing bowl, then stir in the yeast, sugar and ½ teaspoon salt. Make a well in the centre, pour in the oil and about 125 ml (4 fl oz) warm water – enough to bring the dough together. Turn out onto a floured surface and knead for 3 minutes until smooth. Return to the bowl, cover with clingfilm and leave to rise for 1 hour, or until doubled in bulk.

**2** Preheat the oven to gas Mark 6/ 200°C/fan oven 180°C.

**3** Roll the pizza dough out to a 25 cm (10 inches) disc. Transfer to a baking sheet and form a slight lip around the edge of the base to hold in the filling.

**4** Tip the tomatoes into a small saucepan and add the garlic. Simmer for 5 minutes until slightly thickened. Meanwhile, cook the asparagus tips in boiling salted water for 3 minutes then drain well. Spread the tomato sauce over the pizza base, leaving a 2.5 cm (1 inch) border. Scatter the asparagus tips, red pepper, prawns and mozzarella over the pizza.

**5** Bake for 10–12 minutes and serve straight away.

## TIRAMISU

**2 POINTS**

**11 Points per recipe**

Ⓥ *Serves 6*

*Preparation time: 20 minutes plus*
*1 hour chilling*
*Calories per serving: 117*
*Freezing: not recommended*

An utterly delectable mixture of coffee soaked sponge fingers, cool creamy cheese filling and dark chocolate, this elegant dessert is ideal for dinner parties – but your guests certainly won't be able to tell that it's so low in fat.

*200 g (7 oz) Quark*

*200 g (7 oz) very low fat plain fromage frais*

*150 g (5½ oz) low fat custard*

*3 tablespoons granulated sweetener*

*2 teaspoons vanilla extract*

*12 sponge fingers*

*200 ml (7 fl oz) strong black coffee*

*15 g (½ oz) dark chocolate, grated finely*

**1** Whisk the Quark, fromage frais, custard, sweetener and vanilla together until smooth. Place a spoonful of the mixture in each of six serving glasses.

**2** For each tiramisu, dip two sponge fingers in the coffee until just beginning to soften then place in the glass. Cover with the remaining fromage frais mixture. Scatter the grated chocolate on top, cover and chill for at least 1 hour before serving.

## FRUTTI DI BOSCO CHEESECAKE

**3 POINTS**

**32 Points per recipe**

Ⓥ *Serves 10*

*Preparation time: 15 minutes*
*Cooking time: 35 minutes + cooling*
*Calories per serving: 204*
*Freezing: not recommended*

This rich and creamy cheesecake is baked in the oven to give a smooth texture. Frozen summer fruits are used for the 'frutti di bosco' (woodland fruits) topping, but you can also use fresh berries in season, or other tinned fruits such as peaches or mandarins, adjusting the Points as needed.

*110 g (4 oz) digestive biscuits, crushed*

*25 g (1 oz) Grape Nuts cereal*

*40 g (1½ oz) polyunsaturated margarine, melted*

*500 g (1 lb 2 oz) Quark*

*200 g (7 oz) very low fat plain fromage frais*

*60 g (2 oz) caster sugar*

*2 teaspoons vanilla extract*

*3 eggs*

*250 g (9 oz) frozen summer fruits, defrosted*

**1** Preheat the oven to Gas Mark 4/ 180°C/fan oven 160°C.

**2** Mix the biscuit crumbs and cereal with the melted margarine then press into the base of a 20 cm (8 inch) spring form tin. Bake for 8 minutes until firm. Remove from the oven and reduce the temperature to Gas Mark 2/150°C/fan oven 130°C.

**3** Whisk the Quark, fromage frais, sugar, vanilla and eggs together until smooth. Pour onto the biscuit base and bake on the centre shelf for 35 minutes until the filling is set in the centre, but still slightly wobbly. Turn

the oven off but leave the cheesecake in the oven as it cools down. This gradual temperature reduction stops the cheesecake from cracking as it cools.

**4** When at least 2 hours have passed, the cheesecake can be removed from the oven. Once at room temperature, cover and chill in the refrigerator.

**5** Take the cheesecake out of the fridge about 30 minutes before serving to take the chill off it. Carefully remove it from its tin, transfer to a plate and spoon the summer fruits on top. Serve, cut into slices.

**Top tip** The Grape Nuts cereal adds an extra crunch to the base, but you can leave it out if you prefer. The Points per serving will remain the same.

**Frutti di Bosco Cheesecake:** Indulge in this creamy baked cheesecake for only 3 Points per serving.

# tex mex

Tex Mex food is the delicious result of a mingling of Mexican, Native American, Texas cowboy and Anglo cultures in the southwest of the United States. When eating out, extras such as guacamole and soured cream all tend to pile on the Points, but these home-prepared versions cleverly reduce the Points without losing any of the flavour.

## NACHOS WITH SALSA AND GUACAMOLE

**15 Points per recipe**

Ⓥ *Serves 4*

*Preparation and cooking time:*
*25 minutes*

*Calories per serving: 237*

*Freezing: not recommended*

Incorporating Quark into this tasty guacamole means that the Points don't go sky high. Served with No Point tomato salsa and home-baked tortilla chips, this is a great snack for an evening in front of the television.

**For the tortillas**

*4 × 20 cm (8 inches) flour tortillas*

*low fat cooking spray*

*1 teaspoon smoked paprika*

**For the guacamole**

*450 g (1 lb) ripe tomatoes*

*1 medium avocado*

*100 g (3½ oz) Quark*

*1 red onion, finely chopped*

*juice of 1 lime*

*a few drops Tabasco sauce*

**For the salsa**

*2 tablespoons freshly chopped coriander*

*salt and freshly ground black pepper*

**1** Preheat the oven to Gas Mark 4/ 180°C/fan oven 160°C. Spray the tortillas with low fat cooking spray and sprinkle lightly with the smoked paprika. Using kitchen scissors, cut each tortilla into four strips, and then into small triangles. Spread out on a baking tray and bake for 6–7 minutes until golden. Leave to cool and crisp up.

**2** To make the guacamole, cut a small cross in the base of each tomato then place in a bowl and cover with boiling water. Stand for 1 minute then drain and slip off the skins. Quarter and deseed one tomato, then finely dice the flesh. Mash the avocado flesh with the Quark, then mix in the diced tomato, half the red onion and half the lime juice plus Tabasco and seasoning to taste.

**3** To make the salsa, roughly chop the rest of the tomatoes and mix with the coriander, the remaining lime juice and red onion, in a separate bowl.

**4** Serve the tortilla chips with the guacamole and salsa to dip into.

***Top tip*** Smoked paprika, also known as pimentón, has a wonderfully rich smoky flavour, and is sold with the other spices in most major supermarkets. However, ordinary paprika can be used instead.

**Nachos with Salsa and Guacamole:** A great TV snack or perfect for a party at 3½ Points per serving.

**Cajun Potato Wedges:** A classic tex mex restaurant dish for just 3½ Points per serving!

## CAJUN POTATO WEDGES

**7½ Points per recipe**

Ⓥ Serves 2

*Preparation time: 15 minutes*

*Cooking time: 20 minutes*

*Calories per serving: 260*

*Freezing: not recommended*

Great as a starter or side dish, these crispy spicy wedges are perfectly complemented by the cooling soured cream dip and a No Point salsa.

| |
|---|
| 2 × 200 g (7 oz) baking potatoes |
| 1 teaspoon Cajun seasoning |
| low fat cooking spray |
| salt and freshly ground black pepper |
| **For the soured cream dip** |
| 150 g (5½ oz) 0% fat Greek yogurt |
| 2 tablespoons sour cream |
| 1 small garlic clove, crushed |
| 1 tablespoon chopped fresh chives |
| **For the salsa** |
| 10 cherry tomatoes, quartered |
| ½ red pepper, diced finely |
| ½ green chilli, deseeded and chopped finely |
| 1 shallot, chopped finely |
| 1 teaspoon lemon juice |

1 Preheat the oven to Gas Mark 5/ 190°C/fan oven 170°C.

2 Cut each potato into 8 wedges then boil in salted water for 5 minutes. Drain and toss with the Cajun seasoning until evenly coated. Arrange on a baking tray and spray with low fat cooking spray. Bake for 20 minutes (turning half way through) until crisp and golden brown.

3 Mix the salsa ingredients together and set aside for 10 minutes to allow the flavours to develop.

4 Blend together the yogurt, sour cream, garlic, chives and seasoning and serve as a dip for the Cajun wedges.

## BEEF BURRITOS

**20 Points per recipe**

*Serves 4*

*Preparation and cooking time: 20 minutes*

*Calories per serving: 318*

*Freezing: not recommended*

A burrito is a flour tortilla that has been folded and rolled to completely enclose a number of savoury fillings such as meat, re-fried beans, grated cheese, sour cream, lettuce and so on. Here, juicy strips of fillet steak and mushrooms provide a mouth-watering combination.

| |
|---|
| 1½ teaspoons paprika |
| ½ teaspoon ground cumin |
| pinch hot chilli powder |
| 275 g (9½ oz) fillet steak, cut into thin strips |
| 1 teaspoon sunflower oil |
| 1 large onion, sliced |
| 1 clove garlic, crushed |
| 3 large flat mushrooms, sliced |
| 215 g can re-fried beans |
| 4 × 20 cm (8 inch) flour tortillas |
| 4 tablespoons very low fat plain fromage frais |
| ¼ iceberg lettuce, shredded |

1 Mix the spices together and toss the strips of steak in the mixture. Set aside.

2 Heat the oil in a large non-stick frying pan, add the onion and stir-fry for 3 minutes. Add the garlic and mushrooms and cook for 3 minutes until tender. Remove onto a plate.

3 Stir fry the steak strips for 3 minutes over a high heat, then return the onion and mushrooms to the pan and toss everything together. Remove from the heat.

4 Heat the re-fried beans and the tortillas according to the pack instructions.

5 Spread each tortilla with a quarter of the re-fried beans, then divide the steak mixture between them. Top with a tablespoon of fromage frais and shredded lettuce. Roll up the tortillas, folding in the sides to enclose the filling. Serve straightaway.

**Top tip** Very low fat plain fromage frais is a great low Point substitute for soured cream in Tex Mex recipes.

**Variations** Substitute 2 teaspoons Cajun seasoning for the individual spices if you prefer.

For vegetarian mushroom burritos, leave out the steak and use eight large flat mushrooms. The Points will be reduced to 3 per serving.

## PRAWN FAJITAS

**7 Points per recipe**

*Serves 1*

*Preparation and cooking time:*
*15 minutes*

*Calories per serving: 519*

*Freezing: not recommended*

This is a great all-in-one meal for a treat when you are cooking just for yourself, as it's super fast to prepare and looks so colourful and appetizing.

| |
|---|
| 125 g (4½ oz) peeled raw tiger prawns |
| 1 tablespoon lime juice |
| ½ teaspoon Cajun spice |
| 1 teaspoon sunflower oil |
| 1 small red onion, sliced |
| 1 small yellow pepper, deseeded and sliced |

| |
|---|
| 2 × 20 cm (8 inch) flour tortillas |
| 2 tablespoons very low fat plain fromage frais |
| salt and freshly ground black pepper |

**For the salsa**

| |
|---|
| 1 medium tomato, peeled and diced |
| 1 spring onion, chopped |
| 1 teaspoon lime juice |
| a few drops of Tabasco |
| 1 tablespoon fresh coriander, chopped |

**1** Toss the prawns with the lime juice and Cajun spice.

**2** Make the salsa by mixing together all the salsa ingredients with some seasoning.

**3** Heat the oil in a non-stick frying pan, add the onion and pepper and fry for 3 minutes until beginning to colour. Add the prawns and stir-fry for 3 minutes until the prawns are pink and cooked through.

**4** Warm the tortillas for 15 seconds on full power in the microwave or for 20 seconds on each side in a dry frying pan. Divide the prawn and pepper mixture between the tortillas, top with the salsa and fromage frais, roll up and eat immediately!

**Top tip** Any remaining flour tortillas from an opened pack can be individually wrapped and frozen for up to one month. Try using them wrapped around fillings for a packed lunch, instead of a sandwich.

**Variation** For chicken fajitas, cut 100 g (3½ oz) skinless, boneless chicken breast into thin strips to use in place of the prawns. The Points will remain the same.

## SPICY BEAN QUESADILLAS

**27 Points per recipe**

 *Serves 4*

*Preparation and cooking time:*
*25 minutes*

*Calories per serving: 464*

*Freezing: not recommended*

A quesadilla is a Mexican version of a toasted sandwich, using soft flour tortillas instead of bread. Packed with spicy beans and Cheddar cheese, these vegetarian quesadillas are a quick and very nutritious meal, delicious served with a No Point mixed salad.

| |
|---|
| 8 × 20 cm (8 inch) flour tortillas |
| 420 g can mixed beans in chilli sauce |
| 100 g (3½ oz) half fat mature Cheddar cheese, grated |
| ½ red onion, sliced thinly |
| 150 g (5½ oz) mushrooms, sliced |
| 1 red or yellow pepper, diced |
| 1 red chilli, deseeded and sliced |
| 2 tablespoons chopped fresh coriander |

**1** Place a large non-stick frying pan on the hob to preheat.

**2** Meanwhile, lay a tortilla flat on a chopping board, spread a quarter of the beans over the tortilla, then sprinkle with a quarter of the cheese, onion, mushrooms, pepper, chilli and coriander. Top with a second tortilla.

**3** Transfer to the pan and cook over a medium heat for 2 minutes then carefully flip the quesadilla over with the help of a fish slice and cook for 1 minute more.

**4** Repeat with the remaining tortillas and filling ingredients. Serve the quesadillas cut into wedges.

**Variation** Top the cooked quesadillas with 1 tablespoon of very low fat plain fromage frais. The Points will then be 7 per serving.

**Prawn Fajitas:**
These are so
quick and easy
to prepare and
for 7 Points
taste simply
amazing!

**Chilli Beef Tacos:** Great fun for all the family and just 6½ Points per serving.

## CHILLI BEEF TACOS

**26½ Points per recipe**

Serves 4

Preparation time: 20 minutes

Cooking time: 30 minutes

Calories per serving: 434

Freezing: recommended for chilli only

These 'fill your own' tacos make great family food, to be eaten with the hands – messy but a lot of fun!

**For the chilli**

350 g (12 oz) extra lean minced beef

low fat cooking spray

1 large onion, chopped

1 red and 1 green pepper, deseeded and diced

2 garlic cloves, crushed

¼ teaspoon hot chilli powder

1 teaspoon ground cumin

400 g can chopped tomatoes

200 g canned kidney beans, rinsed and drained

200 ml (7 fl oz) beef stock

**To serve**

8 taco shells

½ Iceberg lettuce, shredded

75 g (2¾ oz) half fat mature Cheddar cheese, grated

1  Brown the mince in a flameproof casserole dish in two batches, removing to a plate when done.

2  Spray the casserole dish with low fat cooking spray, then fry the onion, peppers and garlic for 5 minutes. Add the mince and remaining chilli ingredients to the pan. Bring to a simmer, cover and cook gently for 30 minutes.

3  Warm the taco shells for 1 minute on full power in the microwave or for 3 minutes in an oven preheated to Gas Mark 4/180°C/fan oven 160°C. Put some lettuce in each taco, top with the chilli and cheese and serve.

**Variation** For a vegetarian version, substitute Quorn mince for the beef mince, and use vegetable stock. The Points will then be 4½ per serving.

## CHICKEN ENCHILADAS

**29 Points per recipe**

Serves 4

Preparation time: 30 minutes

Cooking time: 25 minutes

Calories per serving: 523

Freezing not recommended

Enchiladas are a classic Tex Mex food, made by wrapping a tortilla around a meat and cheese filling, then baked, topped with a spicy tomato sauce and extra cheese. Serve them with a crisp and crunchy No Point green salad.

300 g (10½ oz) skinless chicken breasts

300 ml (½ pint) hot chicken stock

low fat cooking spray

1 onion, chopped

1 green pepper, deseeded and diced

30 g sachet taco seasoning mix

250 g (9 oz) low fat natural cottage cheese, sieved

75 g (2¾ oz) half fat mature Cheddar cheese, grated finely

500 ml (18 fl oz) passata

¼ teaspoon hot chilli powder

2 garlic cloves, crushed

8 × 20 cm (8 inch) flour tortillas

1  Simmer the chicken breasts in the hot stock for 15 minutes, until completely cooked through. Reserving the liquid, remove the chicken and allow to cool, then tear the meat into thin shreds.

2  Preheat the oven to Gas Mark 4/180°C/fan oven 160°C.

3  Heat the low fat cooking spray in a non-stick pan, add the onion and pepper and cook for 5 minutes until softened. Stir in the shredded chicken, taco seasoning and chicken poaching liquid. Cover and simmer for 10 minutes.

4  Mix the sieved cottage cheese with half of the grated cheese and set aside.

5  Heat the passata, chilli powder and garlic together in a pan and simmer for 10 minutes.

6  Warm the tortillas for 15 seconds on full power in the microwave or for 20 seconds each side in a dry frying pan. Place an eighth of the chicken filling down the centre of each tortilla and spoon an eighth of the cottage cheese mixture on top. Roll up and place in an ovenproof dish, seam side down.

7  Pour the chilli tomato sauce over the filled tortillas and scatter the remaining cheese on top. Bake for 25 minutes.

8  Serve two enchiladas per person.

**Top tips** If you are making the filled tortillas in advance, place them in the baking dish, cover and chill until needed, then top with the tomato sauce and cheese just before cooking so that they don't go soft.

If you have leftover roast chicken, use 200 g (7 oz) for this recipe. The Points will remain the same.

**Variation** For a vegetarian version, use 250 g (9 oz) Quorn mince in place of the cooked chicken and vegetable stock. The Points will remain the same.

1 Preheat the oven to Gas Mark 4/ 180°C/fan oven 160°C, and grease and line 2 × 18 cm (7 inch) cake tins with baking paper.

2 Beat the margarine, sugar, vanilla extract and 1 egg white together for 2 minutes using an electric whisk, until pale and smooth. Gradually beat in the yogurt.

3 Sift the flour, cocoa powder, baking powder, bicarbonate of soda and a pinch of salt together. Add a third of these dry ingredients to the wet, followed by half the milk. Beat until smooth, then whisk in the remaining flour mixture and milk. Fold in two thirds of the grated chocolate.

4 Clean the beaters then whisk the remaining 2 egg whites to soft peaks in another bowl. Whisk in the caster sugar until shiny. Using a large metal spoon, stir a spoonful of egg whites into the cake batter to loosen it and then carefully fold in the remainder.

5 Divide the batter between the prepared tins and bake on the centre shelf for 18–20 minutes, or until risen and springy in the centre. Turn out onto a wire rack to cool.

6 To make the icing, simply beat the icing ingredients together until smooth. Sandwich the cakes together with a third of the icing then spread the remainder over the top and sides. Scatter with the reserved grated chocolate.

**Top tip** Use a really good quality dark chocolate with at least 50% cocoa solids (check the ingredients panel) rather than ordinary cooking chocolate, to give this cake its depth of flavour.

**Devil's Food Cake: A decadent delight but only 3 Points per serving.**

## DEVIL'S FOOD CAKE

**30¹/₂ Points per recipe**

Ⓥ *Serves 10*

*Preparation time: 25 minutes*

*Cooking time: 20 minutes*

*Calories per serving: 197*

*Freezing: recommended for sponge only*

Deliciously damp and dense, it's hard to believe that such an intensely chocolatey cake could be so low in Points, but it really is true. This is a perfect birthday or celebration cake for a chocoholic!

| |
|---|
| 40 g (1¹/₂ oz) polyunsaturated margarine |
| 100 g (3¹/₂ oz) light brown soft sugar |
| 1 teaspoon vanilla extract |
| 3 egg whites |
| 5 tablespoons low fat plain yogurt |
| 150 g (5¹/₂ oz) self raising flour |
| 25 g (1 oz) cocoa powder |
| ¹/₂ teaspoon baking powder |
| ¹/₂ teaspoon bicarbonate of soda |
| 150 ml (5 fl oz) skimmed milk |
| 25 g (1 oz) finely grated dark chocolate |
| 25 g (1 oz) caster sugar |
| salt |

**For the icing**

| |
|---|
| 200 g extra light cream cheese |
| 3 tablespoons granulated sweetener |
| 2 tablespoons cocoa powder, sifted |

## ICE CREAM COOKIE SANDWICH

**4 POINTS**

**33½ Points per recipe**

Ⓥ Serves 8

Preparation time: 10 minutes

Cooking time: 10 minutes

Calories per serving: 222

Freezing: not recommended

In this typically American dessert, chewy cookies are sandwiched together with low fat ice cream – cool and delicious!

75 g (2¾ oz) polyunsaturated margarine

75 g (2¾ oz) caster sugar

1 egg, beaten

½ teaspoon vanilla extract

110 g (4 oz) plain flour

½ teaspoon baking powder

pinch of salt

10 g ground almonds

25 g (1 oz) milk chocolate chips

1 tablespoon skimmed milk

**To serve**

8 scoops low fat vanilla ice cream

**1** Preheat the oven to Gas Mark 4/ 180°C/fan oven 160°C. Line two baking sheets with baking paper.

**2** Cream the margarine and sugar together until pale and fluffy. Gradually beat in the egg and vanilla. Sift the flour, baking powder and salt together and fold into the mixture, followed by the ground almonds, chocolate chips and milk.

**3** Place 8 spoonfuls of cookie mixture on each lined tray, leaving room between them to allow for spreading as they cook. Use the back of a spoon to flatten each spoonful into a 6 cm (2½ inch) disc.

**4** Bake for 10–12 minutes until light golden brown. Cool on the baking sheets for 5 minutes then transfer to a cooling rack.

**5** When cold, sandwich pairs of cookies around a scoop of vanilla ice cream and serve immediately.

**Top tip** If you want to bake these cookies for the biscuit tin, they work out at 3 Points for two.

Ice Cream Cookie Sandwich: Simply scrumptious for 4 Points per serving.

# oriental

Oriental cuisines lend themselves extremely well to Time To Eat with their emphasis on healthy stir frying, small amounts of protein and lots of No Point vegetables that also make them look really colourful and appetizing. In this chapter you'll find some of the most popular Chinese take away choices, from Sweet and Sour Prawns and Beef with Peppers and Black Bean Sauce to Chicken Chow Mein, as well as Thai and Japanese delights.

## SALMON NOODLE BOWL

**5½ Points per recipe**
*Serves 1*
*Preparation and cooking time:*
*15 minutes*
*Calories per serving: 454*
*Freezing: not recommended*

Many people associate Japanese food with sushi and raw fish but there's a huge variety of less daunting cooked dishes as well. This seared salmon noodle bowl is an excellent example of this delicate and refined cuisine.

**For the marinade**

*2 tablespoons teriyaki sauce*

*1 teaspoon granulated sweetener*

*juice of ½ a lime*

**For the salmon and noodles**

*125 g (4½ oz) salmon fillet, skinned*

*30 g (1¼ oz) thin rice noodles*

*425 ml (15 fl oz) fish or chicken stock*

*60 g (2 oz) sugar snap peas, sliced*

*60 g (2 oz) beansprouts, rinsed*

*40 g (1½ oz) drained bamboo shoots*

*1 tablespoon freshly chopped coriander*

*½ red chilli, deseeded and sliced*

*2 spring onions, sliced*

*wedge of lime, to serve*

**1** Mix the teriyaki sauce, granulated sweetener and lime juice together in a dish. Turn the salmon in the marinade to coat and set aside while you prepare the other ingredients.

**2** Soak the rice noodles in boiling water for 5 minutes or according to pack instructions, then drain.

**3** Heat a non-stick frying pan. Lift the salmon out of its marinade (reserving the marinade) then dry fry for 2½ minutes on each side until the flesh is richly caramelised.

**4** Meanwhile, bring the stock to the boil, add the reserved marinade and sugar snap peas and simmer for 3 minutes until just tender.

**5** Place the noodles in a deep bowl. Top with the beansprouts and bamboo shoots. Pour the hot broth and sugar snaps into the bowl and scatter with the coriander, chilli and spring onions. Place the seared salmon on top of the noodles. Serve with a wedge of lime to squeeze over.

**Variations** The salmon can be replaced with a 125 g (4½ oz) skinless chicken breast or 150 g (5½ oz) pork tenderloin if you prefer, but remember these will need about 10 minutes to cook through. The Points will be 3½ per serving for chicken and 4½ for pork.

**Salmon Noodle Bowl:** A wonderful Japanese-style noodle bowl that makes a great all-in-one meal for 5½ Points.

**Vegetable Spring Rolls with Sweet Chilli Sauce:** A fantastic starter for only 1½ Points per serving.

## VEGETABLE SPRING ROLLS WITH SWEET CHILLI SAUCE

**1½ POINTS**

**5½ Points per recipe**

Ⓥ Ⓥⓔ *Serves 4*

*Preparation time: 15 minutes*
*Cooking time: 15 minutes*
*Calories per serving: 166*
*Freezing: recommended*

A pack of ready prepared stir fry vegetables makes light work for these crispy little spring rolls. If you prefer, use the same weight of mixed No Point vegetables such as carrots, peppers, onions, bean sprouts and Chinese leaf, cut into thin shreds.

---

*low fat cooking spray*
*300 g (10½ oz) No Point stir fry vegetables*
*1 teaspoon grated root ginger*
*2 garlic cloves, crushed*
*¼ teaspoon Chinese Five spice powder*
*1 tablespoon soy sauce*
*110 g (4 oz) water chestnuts, drained and sliced*
*Four 25 × 50 cm (10 × 20 inch) sheets filo pastry*
*2 teaspoons sunflower oil*
*1 teaspoon sesame oil*

**For the sauce**
*1 tablespoon soy sauce*
*3 tablespoons sweet chilli sauce*
*juice of ½ a lime*

---

**1** Heat a wok or large non-stick frying pan. Lightly coat with low fat cooking spray then stir fry the vegetables, ginger, garlic and Chinese Five spice powder for 2 minutes. Add the soy sauce and water chestnuts and remove the pan from the heat. Leave to cool slightly.

**2** Preheat the oven to Gas Mark 6/ 200°C/fan oven 180°C.

**3** Cut each sheet of filo in half width ways. Stack the pieces of filo together and keep them covered with a clean damp tea towel while you work.

**4** Mix the sunflower oil and sesame oil together in a small bowl. Take a piece of filo and brush lightly with the blended oil. Fold it in half to give a long narrow rectangle, then place a spoonful of vegetables at one end. Roll up the pastry, folding in the sides to hold in the filling. Place on a baking sheet. Repeat with the rest of the filo sheets and filling to make eight spring rolls, then brush the rolls with any remaining oil.

**5** Bake for 13–15 minutes until crisp and golden. Mix the sauce ingredients together and serve with the spring rolls.

---

## CHICKEN AND SWEETCORN SOUP

**2 POINTS**

**8 Points per recipe**

*Serves 4*
*Preparation and cooking time: 15 minutes*
*Calories per serving: 174*
*Freezing: not recommended*

---

*100 g (3½ oz) baby corn, sliced thinly*
*850 ml (1½ pints) hot chicken stock*
*418 g can creamed sweetcorn*
*150 g (5½ oz) skinless cooked chicken, diced*
*1 tablespoon dry sherry*
*1 egg, beaten*
*2 spring onions, sliced finely*

---

**1** Cook the sliced baby corn in the boiling stock for 5 minutes, then add the creamed corn and diced chicken and simmer for a further 5 minutes.

**2** Add the sherry then pour in the beaten egg, stirring the soup so that the egg forms little threads. Remove the pan from the heat, cover and leave to stand for 2 minutes.

**3** Ladle into bowls and scatter the spring onions on top.

**Variation** For crab and sweetcorn soup, stir a 170g can of white crabmeat, drained, into the soup in place of the chicken. The Points will then be 1½ per serving.

**Chicken and Sweetcorn Soup: A bowlful of this delicate Chinese soup is a comforting treat for just 2 Points.**

## NO POINT VEGETABLE STIR FRY

**0 Points per recipe**

Ⓥ Ⓥⓔ *Serves 2*

*Preparation and cooking time: 15 minutes*

*Calories per serving: 112*

*Freezing: not recommended*

If you've got very few Points left at the end of the day, this fast and fabulous No Point stir fry will come into its own. Serve with a medium portion of rice or noodles (60g/2 oz uncooked weight) for an extra 3 Points.

low fat cooking spray

1 red pepper, sliced thinly

100 g (3½ oz) broccoli, cut into small florets

2 garlic cloves, sliced

1 red chilli, deseeded and sliced

1 teaspoon grated root ginger

½ head Chinese leaf, shredded coarsely

220 g can water chestnuts, drained

2 tablespoons teriyaki sauce

**1** Heat a wok or large non stick frying pan until smoking and spray with low fat cooking spray. Stir fry the pepper and broccoli for 2 minutes, then add the garlic, chilli, ginger and Chinese leaf and cook for a further minute.

**2** Add the water chestnuts, teriyaki sauce and 2 tablespoons of water, cover the pan and steam fry for 2 minutes until the vegetables are just tender. Serve immediately.

**Variation** You can substitute 200 g (7 oz) pak choi for the Chinese leaf if you prefer – the Points will remain the same.

## CHICKEN CHOW MEIN

**5 Points per recipe**

*Serves 1*

*Preparation and cooking time: 20 minutes*

*Calories per serving: 405*

*Freezing not recommended*

This filling noodle dish is a marvellous all in one meal.

50 g (1¾ oz) medium egg noodles

100 g (3½ oz) skinless, boneless chicken breast, cut into thin strips

½ teaspoon sesame oil

low fat cooking spray

1 small onion, sliced

1 garlic clove, sliced

1 teaspoon grated root ginger

60 g (2 oz) beansprouts, rinsed

60 g (2 oz) oyster mushrooms

60 g (2 oz) mange tout

2 tablespoons oyster sauce

**1** Boil the noodles for 5 minutes then rinse in cold water and drain. Toss the chicken with the sesame oil and set aside.

**2** Heat a wok or large non-stick frying pan and spray with low fat cooking spray. Stir fry the onion for 2 minutes, then add the garlic, ginger and chicken and stir fry for a further 3 minutes.

**3** Mix in the beansprouts, mushrooms and mange tout and cook for 2 minutes. Stir in the cooked noodles, oyster sauce and 2 tablespoons of water. Heat through, stirring well for 2 minutes. Serve immediately.

## BEEF WITH PEPPERS AND BLACK BEAN SAUCE

**9½ Points per recipe**

*Serves 2*

*Preparation and cooking time: 15 minutes*

*Calories per serving: 298*

*Freezing: not recommended*

The salty savoury flavour of black bean sauce works particularly well with beef, and fresh red chilli gives this an extra kick. Serve over a medium portion of cooked noodles for an extra 3 Points.

2 teaspoons sunflower oil

250 g (9 oz) pack lean beef fillet steak, cut into strips

1 onion, sliced

1 green pepper, deseeded and roughly chopped

1 garlic clove, sliced

1 cm (½ inch) root ginger, cut into matchsticks

1 red chilli, deseeded and sliced

120 g sachet black bean sauce (see note)

**1** Heat the oil in a wok or large non stick frying pan, until smoking hot. Add the beef strips and onion and stir fry for 2 minutes.

**2** Add all the remaining ingredients except for the black bean sauce and stir fry for 3 minutes.

**3** Pour in the black bean sauce along with 2 tablespoons water and heat through. Serve straight away.

**Note** Black bean sauce is available in sachets from most supermarkets.

# THAI RED CHICKEN CURRY

**11½ Points per recipe**

Serves 4

Preparation and cooking time:
30 minutes

Calories per serving: 194

Freezing: not recommended

Making your own Thai curry paste doesn't take long at all, and the flavour it imparts is simply incomparable. However, if you want to use 2 tablespoons ready-made Thai red curry paste instead, this will alter the Points to 3½ per serving. Serve with a medium portion of cooked rice (60 g/2 oz dried weight) for an extra 3 Points.

### For the red curry paste

½ red onion, peeled

1 red chilli, deseeded and sliced

1 small stick lemongrass, sliced thinly

grated zest and juice of ½ a lime

2.5 cm (1 inch) root ginger, peeled and sliced

1 garlic clove, peeled

1 tablespoon Thai fish sauce

### For the curry

4 dried lime leaves (optional)

150 g (5½ oz) baby corn, sliced

150 g (5½ oz) sugar snap peas

low fat cooking spray

350 g (12 oz) skinless chicken breast, diced

6 spring onions, cut into thirds

200 ml (7 fl oz) reduced fat coconut milk

200 ml (7 fl oz) chicken stock

1 teaspoon light brown soft sugar

110 g (4 oz) cherry tomatoes, halved

chopped fresh coriander to garnish

**1** Place the curry paste ingredients in a food processor or blender and blend until finely chopped.

**2** Soak the lime leaves (if using) in boiling water for 5 minutes and then cut into fine shreds.

**3** Boil the baby corn and sugar snaps for 3 minutes then drain and set aside.

**4** Spray a wok or large non-stick frying pan with low fat cooking spray. Stir fry the chicken and spring onions for 3 minutes, then add the curry paste and fry for 1 minute.

**5** Blend in the coconut milk and chicken stock then add the shredded lime leaves (if using), sugar and blanched vegetables. Simmer gently for 3 minutes, then add the cherry tomatoes and cook for 2 minutes before ladling into warmed bowls. Garnish with chopped coriander.

*Top tip* Dried lime leaves are available in the spice section of most supermarkets. They add a wonderful perfumed fragrance to Thai food.

*Variations* To make green Thai curry paste, substitute a green chilli for the red, regular onion in place of the red onion, and add 2 tablespoons of freshly chopped coriander.

For a vegetarian Thai curry, use light soy sauce in the curry paste instead of fish sauce, vegetable stock rather than chicken, and then add 350 g (12 oz) cooked diced sweet potato in place of the chicken, adding it at step 5. The Points will be reduced to 2½ per serving.

**Thai Red Chicken Curry:
A deliciously fragrant dish for just 3 Points per serving.**

Pad Thai Noodles: A classic Thai dish for only 5½ Points per serving.

## PAD THAI NOODLES

**10½ Points per recipe**

Serves 2

Preparation and cooking time:
25 minutes

Calories per serving: 413

Freezing: not recommended

These stir fried noodles are a staple
Thai dish. They are a great all-in-one
meal, incorporating noodles, chicken,
prawns and egg, stir-fried in a wok
with a sweet-sharp sauce, then
served topped with a crunchy
colourful garnish. Delicious!

| |
| --- |
| 100 g (3½ oz) wide rice noodles |
| low fat cooking spray |
| 100 g (3½ oz) skinless, boneless chicken breast, chopped finely |
| 3 shallots, sliced |
| 2 garlic cloves, crushed |
| ¼ teaspoon crushed dried chillies |
| 2 tablespoons Thai fish sauce |
| 1 tablespoon granulated sweetener |
| juice of 1 lime |
| 150 g (5½ oz) beansprouts, rinsed |
| 60 g (2 oz) small prawns |
| 1 egg, beaten |

**For the garnish**

| |
| --- |
| 2 spring onions, chopped |
| 5 cm (2 inches) cucumber, diced finely |
| ½ red chilli, deseeded and sliced |
| 2 tablespoons chopped fresh coriander |
| 15 g (½ oz) salted peanuts, chopped finely |

1  Soak the rice noodles in boiling
water for 5 minutes or according to
pack instructions, stirring them to
separate the strands. Drain and rinse
well in cold water.

2  Heat the low fat cooking spray in
a wok or large non-stick frying pan
until smoking. Add the chicken,
shallots, garlic and crushed chillies
and stir fry for 3 minutes.

3  Mix the fish sauce, sweetener and
lime juice together then pour into the
pan, quickly followed by the beansprouts and drained noodles. Toss
everything together well and cook
for 1 minute then stir in the prawns
and cook for a further minute.

4  Drizzle the egg over the noodles
and leave to set for about 1 minute.

5  Mix the garnish ingredients
together then add half to the pan.
Give everything one final mix
together then serve in warmed
bowls, topped with the remainder
of the garnish.

**Variation** For a vegetarian version of
Pad Thai, use 150 g (5½ oz) firm
tofu, shredded, in place of the
chicken and prawns, and use light
soy sauce instead of the fish sauce.
The Points will be 5 per serving.

## SPECIAL FRIED RICE

**6 Points per recipe**

Serves 1

Preparation and cooking time:
15 minutes

Calories per serving: 432

Freezing: not recommended

A delicious one-pan meal that can be
adapted to make use of whatever
ingredients you have in the fridge.
To make simple egg fried rice, leave
out the prawns and ham, which will
make it 5 Points per serving, and
serve as an accompaniment to other
stir fried dishes, such as the No Point
Vegetable Stir Fry (p 48).

| |
| --- |
| 60 g (2 oz) rice |
| low fat cooking spray |
| 60 g (2 oz) button mushrooms, sliced |
| 1 garlic clove, crushed |
| 3 spring onions, sliced |
| 1 egg, beaten |
| 40 g (1½ oz) frozen peas, defrosted |
| 40 g (1½ oz) small prawns |
| 25 g (1 oz) wafer thin ham, shredded |
| ½ tablespoon light soy sauce |

1  Cook the rice until tender then
rinse it thoroughly in cold water.

2  Spray a non-stick frying pan or
wok with the low fat cooking spray.
Add the mushrooms, garlic and
spring onions and cook for 2 minutes.

3  Pour in the egg and stir briskly so
that it forms little clumps. Tip in the
rice, peas, prawns, ham and soy
sauce and stir fry for 3 minutes until
thoroughly heated through.

**Top tip** Fried rice works best when
the rice is cooked and cold, as it is
less likely to break up.

**Special Fried
Rice: Packed
full of tasty
ingredients
for 6 Points
per serving.**

## THAI FISHCAKES WITH CUCUMBER DIPPING SAUCE

**6 Points per recipe**

Serves 4

Preparation time: 20 minutes

Cooking time: 10 minutes

Calories per serving: 118

Freezing: recommended for fishcakes only

Although these fragrant little fishcakes are usually served as a starter in Thai restaurants, they make a great low Point main course served with steamed broccoli and 4 tablespoons of cooked rice for an extra 3 Points per serving.

### For the sauce

2 tablespoons soy sauce

1 tablespoon granulated sweetener

4 cm (1½ inches) cucumber, diced finely

grated zest and juice of 1 lime

2 tablespoons chopped fresh coriander

1 red chilli, deseeded and diced finely

2.5 cm (1 inch) root ginger, peeled and sliced

1 stalk lemongrass, chopped roughly

1 tablespoon Thai fish sauce

400 g (14 oz) skinless haddock fillet, diced

1 egg white

1 tablespoon cornflour

60 g (2 oz) green beans, trimmed and sliced thinly

low fat cooking spray

1 Mix the soy sauce, sweetener and cucumber together with 1 tablespoon each of lime juice and chopped coriander and half the diced chilli. Set aside.

2 Place the lime zest and remaining juice in a food processor with the rest of the coriander and chilli, the ginger, lemongrass and fish sauce. Whiz together until finely chopped, then add the fish and pulse together until well blended but not over processed. Scrape the mixture into a bowl and stir in the egg white, cornflour and green beans until thoroughly combined.

3 Using damp hands, shape the mixture into 12 fishcakes. Heat a non-stick frying pan and spray with low fat cooking spray. Cook the fishcakes in two batches for 2½ minutes on each side. Serve with the cucumber dipping sauce.

**Top tip** Using wet hands makes it easier to shape sticky mixtures without getting too messy.

**Variation** You can use other boneless white fish such as coley or hoki in place of the haddock. The Points will remain the same.

## SWEET AND SOUR PRAWNS

**11 Points per recipe**

Serves 4

Preparation and cooking time: 20 minutes

Calories per serving: 239

Freezing: not recommended

Sweet and sour is a favourite Chinese take away dish that is very simple to make at home – for far fewer Points! Serve with 4 tablespoons of cooked rice for an extra 3 Points per serving.

227 g can pineapple pieces in fruit juice

1 tablespoon cornflour

4 tablespoons cider vinegar

2 tablespoons soy sauce

1 tablespoon tomato purée

25 g (1 oz) light brown soft sugar

1 tablespoon vegetable oil

1 onion, sliced

1 red and 1 green pepper, deseeded and diced

2 large carrots, peeled and cut into matchsticks

300 g (10½ oz) frozen raw peeled king prawns, defrosted

220 g can bamboo shoots, drained

1 Drain the juice from the pineapple into a jug, and whisk together with the cornflour, vinegar, soy sauce, tomato purée and sugar. Set the sauce aside.

2 Heat the oil in a wok or large non-stick frying pan until smoking hot. Stir-fry the onion, peppers and carrots for 4 minutes, then stir in the prawns, bamboo shoots and pineapple pieces. Stir fry for a further 2 minutes.

3 Pour in the sauce and 100 ml (3½ fl oz) water, bring to the boil and simmer, stirring until the sauce is thickened but clear. Serve immediately.

**Variation** For sweet and sour chicken, add 350 g (12 oz) diced chicken breast in place of the prawns, but stir fry for 4 minutes to cook the chicken through before adding the sauce. The Points will remain the same.

## CHICKEN AND CASHEW NUTS

**13½ Points per recipe**

Serves 4

Preparation and cooking time:
30 minutes

Calories per serving: 260

Freezing: not recommended

Toasted cashew nuts give this colourful stir fry an extra crunch. As with all stir fried dishes, make sure everything is prepared before you actually start to cook, as the pace is fast and furious! Serve with 4 tablespoons of cooked rice, adding an extra 3 Points per serving.

1 teaspoon sunflower oil

40 g (1½ oz) cashew nuts, halved

350 g (12 oz) skinless, boneless chicken breast, diced

2 teaspoons sesame oil

2 medium carrots, peeled and cut into thin batons

150 g (5½ oz) baby corn, cut into thirds

100 g (3½ oz) mange tout, halved

2 garlic cloves, sliced

1 bunch spring onions, cut into 2.5cm (1 inch lengths), reserving some, finely sliced, for garnishing

2 tablespoons soy sauce

1 tablespoon dry sherry

½ pint (300 ml) chicken stock

1 tablespoon cornflour

**1** Heat the sunflower oil in a wok or a large non-stick frying pan and gently brown the cashew nuts. Remove with a draining spoon and keep to one side.

**2** Coat the chicken in the sesame oil then tip into the hot wok and cook for 3 minutes, stirring occasionally, until browned.

**3** Add the carrots, baby corn, mange tout and garlic and stir fry for 2 minutes.

**4** Stir in the spring onions, soy sauce and sherry and cook for 1 minute.

**5** Return the cashew nuts to the wok, add the chicken stock, cover and simmer for 5 minutes.

**6** Blend the cornflour with one

tablespoon of cold water, then stir into the sauce until slightly thickened. Serve immediately.

**Variation** For a vegetarian version, swap the chicken breast with the same weight of Quorn pieces, and use vegetable stock instead of chicken. The Points will then be 3 per serving.

Chicken and Cashew Nuts: A colourful Oriental stir fried dish, all for just 3½ Points per serving.

---

## LYCHEE GRANITA

**4 Points per recipe**

 Serves 4

Preparation time: 5 minutes plus approx 4 hours freezing

Calories per serving: 75

Freezing: recommended

This fragrant tropical fruit ice is a doddle to make, and provides a very refreshing end to a meal.

425 g can lychees in syrup

3 tablespoons granulated sweetener

juice of 1 lime

4 × mint sprigs to garnish

**1** Tip the lychees and their syrup into a liquidizer and process until smooth. Blend in the sweetener and lime juice.

**2** Pour into a shallow lidded plastic box and freeze for 1-2 hours until the mixture starts to solidify.

**3** Remove from the freezer and stir

well with a fork to break up the large ice crystals. Return to the freezer for 1 hour, then repeat the process. Freeze until firm.

**4** Spoon into individual glasses to serve, garnished with a sprig of mint.

**Top tips** A granita is similar to a sorbet, but has a looser, more granular texture.

The time the granita will take to freeze depends on your freezer.

# indian

With our changing tastes in food, Indian cuisine is now among the most popular British take aways. However, it's also one of the highest Pointed kinds of restaurant food, due to the use of lots of ghee or oil, as well as coconut cream and nuts. But don't despair, with the recipes in this chapter you can still treat yourself to a Friday night curry without having to worry about the Points.

## PRAWN MASALA

**4½ Points per recipe**

*Serves 1*
*Preparation and cooking time:*
*20 minutes*
*Calories per serving: 340*
*Freezing: not recommended*

Coconut essence is a clever way of introducing depth of flavour to a recipe, without adding any of the Points usually associated with coconut products. You can find it in the baking section at the supermarket, with the food colourings and flavourings. It is very concentrated so only add a drop at a time so as not to overdo it. Serve with 4 tablespoons of plain boiled rice for an extra 3 Points.

| |
|---|
| *1 teaspoon sunflower oil* |
| *1 small onion, chopped finely* |
| *1 garlic clove, crushed* |
| *½ teaspoon black onion seeds* |
| *1½ teaspoons hot curry powder* |
| *2 medium tomatoes, halved and grated (see tip)* |
| *2 teaspoons tomato purée* |
| *125 g (4½ oz) peeled raw tiger prawns* |
| *3 drops coconut essence* |

**To serve**

| |
|---|
| *1 tablespoon desiccated coconut* |
| *freshly chopped coriander* |

1 Heat the oil in a saucepan, add the onion and cook for 3 minutes until golden.

2 Add the garlic and spices, followed by the grated tomato, tomato purée and 100 ml (3½ fl oz) water. Simmer for 8 minutes until slightly reduced.

3 Stir in the prawns and the coconut essence and cook for 3 minutes, stirring occasionally, until the prawns are pink and cooked through.

4 Toast the desiccated coconut by heating it in a dry non-stick pan for about 2 minutes, shaking occasionally, until it starts to brown.

5 Serve the prawn masala garnished with the toasted coconut and fresh coriander.

**Top tips** Black onion seeds are also known as 'kalonji' and are usually available from the spice section in the supermarket, as well as from Asian food stores.

Grating tomato is a quick and effective way of getting the tomato flesh without having to worry about skinning the tomato.

**Prawn Masala:
An Indian
favourite for
only 4½ Points
per serving.**

## CHICKEN TIKKA KEBABS

**6 Points per recipe**

Serves 2

Preparation time: 15 minutes
+ 30 minutes marinating

Cooking time: 15 minutes

Calories per serving: 245

Freezing: not recommended

If you can leave the chicken to marinate overnight, it will become even more succulent and full of flavour. Serve with a portion of Saag Aloo (see p 63) for an extra 1½ Points.

| |
|---|
| 1 tablespoon hot curry powder |
| ¼ teaspoon turmeric |
| 1 garlic clove, crushed |

| |
|---|
| 1 teaspoon grated root ginger |
| 1 tablespoon lemon juice |
| 100 ml (3½ fl oz) low fat natural yogurt |
| 2 medium skinless, boneless chicken breasts |
| 1 green pepper, deseeded and cut into chunks |
| 1 medium red onion, cut into chunks |
| salt and freshly ground black pepper |

**1** Mix the spices, garlic, ginger, lemon juice and yogurt together until smooth, adding some seasoning. Cut each chicken breast into seven or eight pieces and toss in the yogurt mixture to coat. Cover and chill for at least 30 minutes.

**2** Preheat the grill or barbecue to its highest setting. Thread the marinated chicken onto four short skewers, alternating with pieces of pepper and onion.

**3** Grill or barbecue the kebabs for 15 minutes, turning occasionally, until the chicken is cooked through and slightly charred at the edges.

**Top tip** If you want to achieve the reddish colour of chicken tikka that is found in restaurants where colouring is used, leave the turmeric out of the marinade and add ½ teaspoon of paprika plus 1 tablespoon of tomato purée.

**Variation** For vegetarian tikka kebabs, marinate 16 button mushrooms in the tikka marinade instead of the chicken. These kebabs will take only 8–10 minutes to cook, and will be just ½ Point per serving.

## VEGETABLE SAMOSAS

**6 Points per recipe**

Ⓥ Ⓥᵉ (without the dipping sauce)

Serves 4

Preparation time: 25 minutes

Cooking time: 15 minutes

Calories per serving: 145

Freezing: recommended

These spicy vegetable filled samosas are perfect for a lunchbox. Make a cool dipping sauce by stirring together 100 ml (3½ fl oz) low fat natural yogurt and 2 teaspoons mint sauce – all for 1 Point extra.

| |
|---|
| 250 g (9 oz) potatoes, peeled and diced into 1 cm (½ inch) pieces |
| 200 g (7 oz) carrots, peeled and diced into 1 cm (½ inch) pieces |
| 50 g (1¾ oz) frozen peas |
| low fat cooking spray |

| |
|---|
| 1 teaspoon medium curry powder |
| ½ teaspoon black mustard seeds |
| pinch hot chilli powder |
| 2 tablespoons chopped fresh coriander |
| Four 25 × 50 cm (10 × 20 inch) large sheets filo pastry |
| salt and freshly ground black pepper |

**1** Preheat the oven to Gas Mark 5/190°C/fan oven 170°C.

**2** Cook the diced potatoes and carrots in boiling salted water for 7–8 minutes until tender. Drain.

**3** Tip the frozen peas into a sieve and run under the cold tap to defrost. Spray a non-stick saucepan with low fat cooking spray, add the spices and peas and stir fry for 1 minute. Add the potatoes and carrots and mix together well, lightly crushing some of the vegetables.

**4** Remove from the heat and stir in the coriander and plenty of seasoning. Tip out onto a plate to cool slightly and divide into 8 portions.

**5** Cut each sheet of filo in half width ways. Stack the pieces of filo together and keep them covered with a damp towel while you work.

**6** Take a piece of filo and spray with low fat cooking spray. Fold in half lengthways to give a long narrow strip. Place a spoonful of the spicy vegetables near the top, bring one corner of the pastry down over the filling, then fold the pastry up in a series of triangle shapes. Place the samosa on a baking tray with the end of the pastry tucked underneath.

**7** Repeat with the remaining filo sheets and vegetables.

**8** Spray the samosas with low fat cooking spray, then bake in the oven for 15 minutes until golden brown and crisp. Let them cool slightly before eating.

**Chicken Tikka Kebabs:** Colourful and tasty kebabs for only 3 Points per serving.

**Garlic and Coriander Naan Bread:** Ideal for mopping up the flavoursome sauce of a curry, these breads are just 2½ Points each.

## GARLIC AND CORIANDER NAAN BREAD

 **2½ POINTS**

**21 Points per recipe**

ⓥ *Makes 8*

*Preparation time: 15 minutes +*
*1½ hours rising*

*Cooking time: 5 minutes*

*Calories per serving: 190*

*Freezing: recommended*

These puffy naan breads are an ideal accompaniment to a lovely saucy curry instead of rice, or they can be split open and filled as an alternative to a sandwich.

*400 g (14 oz) plain flour, plus 1 tablespoon for kneading and 1 tablespoon for rolling*

*1 teaspoon fast action yeast*

*1 teaspoon salt*

*150 ml (5 fl oz) low fat natural yogurt*

*2 garlic cloves, crushed*

*3 tablespoons chopped fresh coriander*

**1** Mix the flour with the yeast and 1 teaspoon salt in a large bowl. Make a well in the centre and pour in the yogurt, then add up to 125 ml (4 fl oz) warm water, to bring together as a soft dough. Turn out onto a lightly floured surface and knead for 3 minutes until soft and springy. Stretch out the dough and scatter with the garlic and coriander. Knead again until evenly distributed throughout the dough.

**2** Return the dough to the bowl and cover with cling film. Leave to rise in a warm place for 1½ hours or until doubled in bulk.

**3** Preheat the oven to Gas Mark 8/ 230°C/fan oven 210°C. Place two large baking sheets in the oven to preheat.

**4** Divide the dough into 8 pieces. Roll each one out on a lightly floured surface to an oval shape, measuring about 12 × 18 cm (4½ × 7 inches). Bake the naan bread on the preheated baking sheets for 5 minutes, or until puffy and browned in patches. Serve warm.

***Top tip*** To freeze the naan breads, wrap them individually in cling film once cooled, then freeze in a plastic bag for up to one month.

## TARKA DAHL

**2 POINTS**

**8½ Points per recipe**

Ⓥ Ⓥg Serves 4

Preparation time: 10 minutes

Cooking time: 15 minutes

Calories per serving: 180

Freezing: recommended (at the end of step 2)

'Dahl' is a generic word for lentils, of which many types are used in Indian cuisine, as well as for this thick soupy curry. 'Tarka' is a spiced butter or oil that is added to a dish just before serving. Dahl is usually served as part of a larger spread (in which case it would serve 8 people at 1 Point each), but it makes a hearty meal in its own right, served with a Garlic and Coriander Naan Bread for 2½ Points (see p 58).

150 g (5½ oz) split red lentils, rinsed

1 onion, chopped finely

1 tablespoon grated root ginger

600 ml (1 pint) vegetable stock

2 teaspoons sunflower oil

2 garlic cloves, sliced

½ teaspoon black mustard seeds

½ teaspoon cumin seeds

1 tablespoon tomato purée

1 tablespoon lemon juice

salt and freshly ground black pepper

**To serve**

2 tomatoes, peeled, deseeded and diced

chopped fresh coriander

1 Place the lentils in a saucepan with the onion, ginger and vegetable stock. Bring to the boil and simmer, covered, for 15 minutes until the lentils have absorbed most of the liquid and broken down to a mushy pulp.

2 Heat the oil, garlic, mustard seeds and cumin seeds together in a small pan for 1 minute or until golden (don't let the garlic burn). Stir in the tomato purée and cook for 30 seconds. Add a ladleful of lentils to the pan, stir everything together then return everything to the lentil pan. Stir in the lemon juice and add seasoning to taste.

3 Serve garnished with the diced tomatoes and chopped coriander.

**Top tips** You can turn this into a hearty warming soup, simply by doubling the amount of stock used. The Points will remain the same.

If you enjoy cooking Indian food, it really is worth keeping a stock of some whole spices such as cumin seeds and black mustard seeds, as they have a more intense flavour than ready ground spices.

## CREAMY VEGETABLE AND CHICKPEA KORMA

**4 POINTS**

**16½ Points per recipe**

Ⓥ Ⓥg Serves 4

Preparation time: 20 minutes

Cooking time: 25 minutes

Calories per serving:

Freezing: not recommended

This mild and creamy korma is gently perfumed with aromatic spices rather than being heavy on the chilli content. The combination of sweet butternut squash and succulent peppers with the nuttiness of the chickpeas is simply divine.

2 teaspoons sunflower oil

1 onion, sliced

2 red peppers, deseeded and chopped

1 medium butternut squash, peeled, deseeded and diced

2 garlic cloves, crushed

1 tablespoon grated root ginger

1 tablespoon ground coriander

1 teaspoon cumin seeds

pinch hot chilli powder

25 g (1 oz) ground almonds

250 ml (9 fl oz) vegetable stock

200 ml (7 fl oz) reduced fat coconut milk

110 g (4 oz) green beans, trimmed and cut into thirds

410 g can chickpeas, rinsed and drained

salt and freshly ground black pepper

1 Heat the oil in a large non-stick pan. Fry the onion and peppers for 5 minutes over a medium heat.

2 Add the butternut squash, garlic, ginger and spices and stir until evenly coated. Add the ground almonds, then blend in the vegetable stock and coconut milk. Season to taste then bring to the boil, cover and simmer for 15 minutes.

3 Add the green beans and chickpeas and cook for a further 10 minutes.

**Creamy Vegetable and Chickpea Korma: Delicious and satisfying and only 4 Points.**

## MUSHROOM PILAU

3½ POINTS

**7 Points per recipe**

Ⓥ Ⓥg *Serves 2*

*Preparation time: 10 minutes*

*Cooking time: 15 minutes*

*Calories per serving: 285*

*Freezing: not recommended*

This is a quick and easy vegetable pilau that can be served on its own or with another curry, such as Tarka Dahl (see p 59).

| |
|---|
| 1 medium onion, chopped finely |
| 1 teaspoon sunflower oil |
| 200 g (7 oz) button mushrooms, quartered |
| 1 teaspoon hot curry powder |
| ½ teaspoon cumin seeds |
| ½ teaspoon black mustard seeds |
| 125 g (4½ oz) basmati rice |
| ½ teaspoon salt |

**1** Soften the onion in the oil for 3 minutes, then add the mushrooms and cook for a further 3 minutes. Stir in the spices and rice and cook, stirring, for 1 minute.

**2** Add ½ teaspoon of salt and 300 ml (½ pint) boiling water. Bring to the boil, stir once then cover the pan and cook on a very low heat for 15 minutes, without lifting the lid.

**3** Fluff up the rice with a fork before serving.

**Variation** For a mushroom and pea pilau, add 100 g (3½ oz) frozen peas with the rice, which will increase the Points to 4 per serving.

## LAMB JALFREZI

4 POINTS

**15 Points per recipe**

*Serves 4*

*Preparation time: 15 minutes*

*Cooking time: 10 minutes*

*Calories per serving: 264*

*Freezing: recommended*

This dish is a very popular choice on restaurant menus throughout Great Britain and this low Point version is delicious! Serve with 4 tablespoons cooked rice for an extra 3 Points.

| |
|---|
| low fat cooking spray |
| 500 g (1 lb 2 oz) lean lamb leg steak, cut into strips |
| 1 large onion, sliced |
| 1 red and 1 green pepper, sliced |
| 2 tablespoons Madras curry paste |
| 400 g can chopped tomatoes |
| 2 tablespoons tomato purée |
| 100 ml (3½ fl oz) low fat plain yogurt |

**1** Place a large non-stick frying pan on the hob to preheat. Spray with low fat cooking spray and fry the meat until lightly browned and then remove it to a plate.

**2** Brown the onion and peppers for 5 minutes over a medium heat, then return the meat to the pan. Stir in the curry paste and fry for 30 seconds before adding the tomatoes and tomato purée. Gradually stir in the yogurt and then add 150 ml (5 fl oz) hot water. Bring to the boil and simmer for 10 minutes until the meat and vegetables are tender.

**Variation** Lean turkey breast strips can be used in place of the lamb. The Points will be reduced to 3 per serving.

## CHEAT'S CHICKEN MAKHANI

3½ POINTS

**6½ Points per recipe**

*Serves 2*

*Preparation and cooking time: 20 minutes*

*Calories per serving: 267*

*Freezing: not recommended*

This cheat's version of chicken makhani (butter chicken) might be low in Points, but it's fabulously rich tasting. Stirring in a little butter at the end enriches the sauce wonderfully so don't leave it out. Accompany with a Garlic and Coriander Naan Bread (see p 58) for an extra 2½ Points, to mop up the flavoursome sauce.

| |
|---|
| 230g can chopped tomatoes |
| 1 teaspoon tomato purée |
| 1 teaspoon grated root ginger |
| 2 garlic cloves, crushed |
| ¼ teaspoon hot chilli powder |
| 200 ml (7 fl oz) chicken stock |
| 15 g (½ oz) ground almonds |
| 1 teaspoon caster sugar |
| 225 g pack tandoori chicken breast pieces |
| 1 tablespoon half fat butter |
| ½ teaspoon garam masala |

**1** Place the chopped tomatoes, tomato purée, ginger, garlic, chilli powder and chicken stock in a saucepan. Simmer briskly, uncovered, for 10 minutes to reduce.

**2** Stir in the ground almonds, sugar and tandoori chicken pieces. Gently heat through for 7 minutes, then stir in the butter and garam masala. Serve straightaway.

Cheat's Chicken
Makhani: A truly
authentic tasting
curry for only
3½ Points.

400 g can chopped tomatoes

150 ml (5 fl oz) vegetable stock

100 ml (3½ fl oz) low fat natural
yogurt

1 To make the meatballs process
the onion, garlic, chillies, ginger and
1 tablespoon chopped coriander
together in a food processor until
finely chopped. Add half a teaspoon
of salt, freshly ground black pepper,
the ground cumin, lamb mince and
breadcrumbs and pulse together until
just mixed.

2 Shape into 20 small meatballs then
chill, covered, for 30 minutes.

3 For the sauce, start by softening
the onion in the oil for 3 minutes.

4 Add the spices and cook for 30
seconds before stirring in the
tomatoes and stock. Season and
bring to a simmer, then gradually stir
in the yogurt.

5 Slide in the chilled meatballs and
gently push them down into the
sauce. Cover and simmer gently for
30 minutes, shaking the pan from
time to time to move the meatballs
around. Serve garnished with
chopped fresh coriander.

**Top tip** The meatballs firm up when
chilled which makes them less likely
to break up in the sauce.

**Variation** You can substitute extra
lean minced beef or minced turkey
for the lamb if you prefer. The Points
will be 4 and 3½ respectively.

**Lamb Kofta
Curry: A
delicious curry
for only 5 Points
per serving.**

## LAMB KOFTA CURRY

**5 POINTS**

**19½ Points per recipe**

Serves 4

Preparation time: 20 minutes +
30 minutes chilling

Cooking time: 30 minutes

Calories per serving: 257

Freezing: recommended

These tender meatballs simmered in
a fragrant gravy, make excellent
comfort food with an exotic twist.
Serve with aromatic Mushroom Pilau
at 3½ Points per serving (see p 60),
or with 4 tablespoons of plain boiled
rice for an extra 3 Points.

**For the meatballs**

1 medium onion, quartered

2 garlic cloves, peeled

2 green chillies, deseeded

2.5 cm (1 inch) piece root ginger,
peeled and sliced

1 tablespoon chopped fresh coriander,
plus extra to garnish

½ teaspoon ground cumin

350 g (12 oz) extra lean lamb mince

50 g (1¾ oz) fresh breadcrumbs

salt and freshly ground black pepper

**For the curry sauce**

1 onion, chopped finely

2 teaspoons sunflower oil

2 tablespoons medium curry powder

1 teaspoon cumin seeds

½ teaspoon hot chilli powder

## SAAG ALOO

**6½ Points per recipe**

Ⓥ Ⓥⓖ *Serves 4*

*Preparation and cooking time:*
*25 minutes*

*Calories per serving: 188*

*Freezing: not recommended*

This spicy spinach and potato dish is delicious eaten cold as well as hot, and makes a great filling for a pitta bread in a packed lunch.

| |
| --- |
| *1 medium onion, sliced* |
| *1 tablespoon sunflower oil* |
| *1 teaspoon turmeric* |
| *600 g (1 lb 5 oz) potatoes, peeled and diced* |
| *½ teaspoon hot chilli powder* |
| *1 teaspoon ground cumin* |
| *1 teaspoon black mustard seeds* |
| *1 teaspoon grated root ginger* |
| *230 g can chopped tomatoes* |
| *225 g (8 oz) fresh young leaf spinach, rinsed and drained* |
| *salt* |

**1** Soften the onion in the oil for 10 minutes over a gentle heat.

**2** Bring a pan of salted water to the boil. Add ½ teaspoon turmeric and the potatoes, cover and simmer for 10 minutes until tender.

**3** Stir the remaining spices and ginger into the onions and cook for 1 minute. Add the tomatoes and spinach and cook until the spinach has wilted.

**4** Drain the potatoes and toss with the spinach mixture until combined.

**Variation** For Saag Gobi (spinach and cauliflower), use cauliflower florets instead of the potato. This will be just ½ Point per serving.

## MANGO AND COCONUT POTS

**15½ Points per recipe**

Ⓥ *Serves 6*

*Preparation time: 10 minutes*

*Cooking time: 25 minutes*

*Calories per serving: 133*

*Freezing: not recommended*

The tropical flavours of mango and coconut combine beautifully in these velvety little custard pots.

| |
| --- |
| *1 lime* |
| *425g can mango slices in syrup, drained* |
| *2 eggs plus 2 egg whites* |
| *40 g (1½ oz) caster sugar* |
| *200 ml (7 fl oz) reduced fat coconut milk* |
| *150 ml (5 fl oz) skimmed milk* |
| *few drops coconut essence* |

**1** Preheat the oven to Gas Mark 2/ 150°C/fan oven 130°C.

**2** Remove the lime zest using a zester. Once the zest has been removed, squeeze the juice from the lime. Place the zest in a saucer, cover with damp kitchen paper and reserve for garnish. Finely dice three pieces of the mango for garnish, cover and keep in the fridge.

**3** Place the remaining mango pieces in a liquidizer with the lime juice and blend to a smooth purée.

**4** Whisk the whole eggs, egg whites and caster sugar together in a mixing bowl, then mix in the coconut milk, skimmed milk and mango purée. Add a few drops of coconut essence, then divide the mixture between six ramekins or heatproof teacups.

**5** Place the ramekins in a roasting tin and pour in boiling water from the kettle so that it comes two thirds of the way up the dishes. Bake in the

centre of the oven for 25 minutes until slightly puffy and set.

**6** Remove the ramekin dishes from the roasting tin and leave to cool to room temperature, then cover and chill for at least 2 hours before serving.

**7** Serve topped with the diced mango flesh and a scattering of lime zest.

**Top tip** Left over coconut milk from an opened tin can be frozen in a lidded plastic container, and kept to use in another recipe such as Thai Red Chicken Curry (see p 49) or Creamy Vegetable and Chickpea Korma (see p 59).